MW00780919

Public Speaking for Criminal Justice Professionals

Public Speaking for Criminal Justice Professionals

A Manner of Speaking

Thomas P. Mauriello

CRC Press
Taylor & Francis Group
Boca Raton London New York

CRC Press is an imprint of the
Taylor & Francis Group, an **informa** business

First edition published 2021
by CRC Press
6000 Broken Sound Parkway NW, Suite 300, Boca Raton, FL 33487-2742

and by CRC Press
2 Park Square, Milton Park, Abingdon, Oxon, OX14 4RN

Library of Congress Cataloging-in-Publication Data

Names: Mauriello, Thomas P., author.
Title: Public speaking for criminal justice professionals : a manner of speaking / Thomas Mauriello.
Description: First edition. | Boca Raton : CRC Press, 2020. | Includes bibliographical references and index. | Summary: "Public Speaking for Criminal Justice Professionals: A Manner of Speaking is the first of its kind public speaking guide specifically written for criminal justice professionals, written by a criminal justice professional." --Provided by publisher.
Identifiers: LCCN 2020005379 (print) | LCCN 2020005380 (ebook) | ISBN 9780367498894 (hardback) | ISBN 9780367498863 (paperback) | ISBN 9781003047957 (ebook)
Subjects: LCSH: Criminal justice, Administration of. | Public speaking. | Forensic oratory. | Communication in law. | Communication in law enforcement.
Classification: LCC HV7419 .M38 2020 (print) | LCC HV7419 (ebook) | DDC 808.5/1024364--dc23
LC record available at https://lccn.loc.gov/2020005379
LC ebook record available at https://lccn.loc.gov/2020005380

ISBN: 978-0-367-49889-4 (hbk)
ISBN: 978-0-367-49886-3 (pbk)
ISBN: 978-1-003-04795-7 (ebk)

Typeset in Palatino
by Deanta Global Publishing Services, Chennai, India

This book is dedicated to my family:

To my wife, Laurie; and our children, Scott, Leah, and Katelyn;

their spouses, Whitney, Luiz, and Greg;

our grandsons, Brayden, Trace, and Weston;

our granddaughters, Sophia and Olivia;

and to all our future descendants

CONTENTS

PART II   Special Criminal Justice and Forensic Sciences Presentation Tasks

PART III Evaluating and Fine-Tuning Your Performance

CONTENTS

PREFACE

"It is not enough to know what to say; one must also know how to say it."

– Aristotle: *Politics* (Book 3)

If you are wondering if this book is for you, let me assure you it is. You were interested enough to open its cover and turn to the Preface, so let me invite you to continue to read and learn how you can develop and fine-tune your speaking skills to be a welcomed, competent, and accomplished speaker. "Great public speakers are not born; they are trained."[1] Therefore, you can be as good as you want to be with the right training and practice. So begin right here.

Public Speaking for Criminal Justice Professionals: A Manner of Speaking is a first of its kind public speaking guide specifically written for criminal justice professionals, written by a criminal justice professional. I am the author, Thomas Mauriello. I have paralleled my entire professional career both as a practitioner and as an educator in the fields of criminal justice, counterintelligence, and forensic science. This book shares with you, the reader, the public speaking skills I have learned, used, misused, and taught to thousands of criminal justice, forensic science, security, and counterintelligence professionals and students during my 46 year, and still counting, professional career.

"Most people would generally agree that a great deal – probably most – of the presentations we have to sit through in the professional world are awful. They are all too often passionless, boring, and dense with unreadable PowerPoint slides."[2] That can stop for you right here. The objectives for success in this book are

- To facilitate thought and ideas for an effective, entertaining, and strategically planned oral presentation
- To satisfy the needs and expectations of the audience

- To strengthen the oral communication skills of criminal justice professionals in court, in the classroom, in front of a camera, presenting technical and scientific papers, and when speaking to the general public

It is my experience and belief that poor presentations occur because the speaker has no plan of action or foundation from which to develop a strong presentation that can be heard, understood, and remembered. You must have an organized plan that will follow you through from beginning to end. This book does that for you whether you are an experienced or novice speaker.

This book also improves the reader's presentation skills, whether you are preparing to speak to an audience of one or one thousand. It will enhance the capabilities of the experienced speaker while producing an essential foundation for the beginner. The book includes techniques for speaking with confidence, choosing the right audiovisual technologies, and how-to strategies for satisfying the needs and expectations of any audience. One hundred-plus proven effective presentation "reflection tools" are highlighted and demonstrated throughout the book using illustrated criminal justice and forensic sciences topic examples. The critical reflection tools discussed in each chapter are listed at the end of each chapter section.

Knowing your topic or being an expert in the subject does not guarantee a successful presentation. Aristotle, who many recognize as the "Father of Public Speaking and Forensic Debate," said it best when he declared, "It is not enough to know what to say, one must know how to say it."[3] This book focuses on *technique* rather than *substance* with the recognition that "a speech is composed of three factors – the speaker, the subject and the listener – and it is to the last of these that its purpose is related."[4] What Aristotle was saying is the only reason for a presentation at any level is because of the presence of an audience. Without the audience, the speaker would not exist. Aristotle was also a "storyteller" who used stories of past experiences as a technique to help his listeners understand and remember central ideas and concepts he was discussing in his speeches. You will see a series of "Storytelling" passages in this book that exemplify Aristotle's methodology for learning. They are stories from my public speaking experiences that demonstrate a technique or method discussed in the chapter content.

This book is written to be read from cover to cover by the new speaker or for the experienced speaker who wants to fine-tune their existing oral communication skills. It also can be used as a reference guide to focus on improving specific skills and techniques that need further development. Although written for the criminal justice professional, the basic principles of public speaking are the same for any oral communication undertaking. That means its benefit is not limited to only criminal justice professionals but includes any profession, topic, or venue.

Professionals who don't want to speak in public, or are afraid to speak to groups in general, or believe they are not good at it, tend to shy away from career opportunities that require a significant amount of oral communication. They don't think they can overcome the infliction imposed on themselves, so they don't do it at all or are just satisfied being a mediocre speaker. This book recognizes this to be problematic for the criminal justice professional and offers the reader the ability to integrate a series of tools and a structured plan to present their expertise proficiently. The result is becoming customer-focused with your audience and developing the confidence to present your thoughts, ideas, testimony, evidence, and scientific conclusions in a manner that is noticeably "heard, understood and remembered."

When you are being "heard," you are physically being heard by the entire audience no matter where they are sitting. When you are being "understood," you are speaking in a language and using words that are generally familiar to the audience. For example, you are defining technical terms or acronyms for the audience. Your speech is not a form of communication when you speak; it's communication when you're understood. Finally, and most important, being "remembered" means your presentation is conveyed in such a manner to allow the audience to walk away and recall you and the essential points you made during the presentation.

Joan Minninger, PhD, in her book *Total Recall: How to Maximize Your Memory Power*, tells us that

> Memory is complicated by how we perceive the sights, sounds, and sensations that surround us. The possibilities for variations in encoding are almost infinite. Some things that may affect how we evaluate information are our age, sex, intelligence, education, disposition, our nationality and social status, our political and religious beliefs, our physical appearance, income, the weather, the people around us, where we are, and the time of the day, month, and year.[5]

Public speakers have to consider and deal with all these obstacles to ensure their message is received effectively and accurately. These obstacles are discussed throughout the chapters of this book.

This book provides immediate results for a successful presentation. The 100-plus "Reflection" tools highlighted at the end of each chapter provide quick reference points when preparing a presentation. Thousands of students have used these tools, during and after attending my workshop "Motivation through Communications – A Public Speaking Skills Presentation," delivered to hundreds of audiences worldwide. This book documents those skills and allows you to have them with you as needed.

So let's continue.

Thomas P. Mauriello, M.F.S.
Author, Forensic Consultant, Senior Lecturer

CHAPTER REVIEW REFLECTION TOOLS

1. It is not enough to know what to say; one must also know how to say it.
2. Great public speakers are not born; they are trained.
3. Poor presentations are generally poorly planned.
4. Use Aristotle's storytelling to help your audience remember.
5. A speech is composed of three factors: the speaker, the subject, and the listener.
6. Be heard, understood, and remembered.
7. A speech is not a form of communication when you speak; it's communication when you are understood.

NOTES

1. Quoted by Dale Carnegie, a traveling salesman, before teaching public speaking at a YMCA. His seminal self-help book, *How to Win Friends and Influence People*, won him a national following and enabled him to expand the Dale Carnegie Institute into countries around the world. www.biography.com/writer/dale-carnegie.
2. Nick Morgan, "Why Is Good Public Speaking Important to the Business World?" December 26, 2011, https://publicwords.com/2011/12/26/why-is-good-public-speaking-important-to-the-business-world/.
3. Aristotle, *Politics* (Book 3).
4. Aristotle, *The Art of Rhetoric*, Chapter 1.3, 1358b.
5. Joan Minninger, *Total Recall: How to Maximize Your Memory Power*, MJF Books, 1984, p. 19.

ACKNOWLEDGMENTS

I began my career back in 1973, believing that I would spend my entire professional life as a practitioner. That changed one day in 1976 when I was in the communications center at the police department where I was working. A nonemergency phone line began ringing so I answered it for the dispatcher. It was a professor from the Institute of Criminal Justice and Criminology, University of Maryland, a Dr. Knowlton Johnson. Dr. Johnson asked if a police officer would be willing to be a guest speaker in his Police–Community Relations class that semester. I placed him on hold and frantically ran around trying to find an officer who was willing to speak in his class. No one wanted to do it.

I got back on the phone and apologized to Dr. Johnson, telling him that there was no one available. He asked me if I was a police officer, and I thoughtlessly said yes. I could have told him I was the janitor, but no, I told him the truth. He asked me if I would come to his class and talk about how the police interact with the community. I agreed to go and surprisingly totally enjoyed the first-time experience.

Dr. Johnson told me I did well for my first time as a speaker, and after a few return visits to his class and a developed friendship that has extended to this day, Dr. Johnson got me a job as an adjunct instructor at the University of Maryland. That was 42 years ago. My sincere thanks to Dr. Johnson for his guidance and encouragement to seek a dual career as a criminal justice professional and an educator and speaker. I credit him for introducing me to the world of public speaking that has been the common denominator in every job and assignment I have had throughout my entire career. Thank you, Knowlton.

Jumping ahead to the writing and publication of this book, I want to thank Mark Listewnik, senior editor, CRC Press/Taylor & Francis Group. Mark extended to me the opportunity to write this book and document my public speaking experiences and knowledge, which has been my favorite pastime for all these years. He has guided me through the editorial process that has resulted in the publication of this book.

This is the fourth book I have written, all related to the criminal justice field, and this was the most rewarding of them all. Life is full of opportunities to excel, but I believe writing this book is one of my finest moments. At no time was writing this book a chore. It was written with the same enthusiasm and excitement that I experience each time I speak in public.

I want to thank Aristotle, the Father of Public Speaking, for it was his wisdom he shared back in 350 B.C. when he wrote his book *The Art of Rhetoric*, which has influenced me as a public speaker. He wrote, "a speech is composed of three factors – the speaker, the subject and the listener – and it is to the last of these that its purpose is related."[1] It was in this passage that he taught me the importance of satisfying the audience. I also want to thank Aristotle for his method of "storytelling" to help listeners to understand and remember better. Telling stories that relate to points being made in a speech has proven to me to be a valued method of teaching that I have highlighted in this book.

I want to thank a longtime colleague and close friend, Ray Semko, "The D*I*C*E Man," for allowing me to share with my readers his unique style (his shtick) of speaking in public to gain audience attention and respect. Thanks to Ray and his website designer and creative consultant, Cynthia J. Kwitchoff, I have been able to include several wonderful images that capture Ray at his best, a consummate professional public speaker.

I have another colleague and friend, Rusty Capps, who I consulted with on numerous occasions during the writing of this book. Rusty is one of the country's leading instructors and advocates for counterterrorism, counterintelligence, and security awareness education, which is taken directly from his past experiences as an FBI agent. I thank him for his friendship and the sharing of his expertise during the planning and development stages of this project.

There are numerous images, photographs, and visuals contained in this book that are recognized on the pages where they have been placed. I thank those persons, agencies, universities, and companies who allowed me to use them as demonstrative tools. They include my friend and colleague, Sandra Enslow, lead forensic artist, Los Angeles County Sheriff's Department; and Captain Paul Starks (Retired), Montgomery County Maryland Police Department and also a former student of the author at the University of Maryland. I also would like to thank one of my students, Joshua Smith, who allowed me to use his facial expressions to demonstrate nonverbal communications available to the speaker. He did a great job in this regard, and I appreciate his time and effort. Thank you Josh, and good luck in your future career. And my thanks and appreciation to

Luiz Santos, the photographer who captured Joshua so well and high-lighted many of the key tools illustrated throughout the book.

And finally, I want to thank my two main places of employment: the University of Maryland and the US Department of Defense, for providing me with the time and opportunity to develop and master the oral communication skills that I have been able to share with you in this book.

NOTE

1. Aristotle, *The Art of Rhetoric*, translated with an introduction and notes by H. C. Lawson-Tancred, Penguin Books, 1991, p. 80.

AUTHOR

Thomas P. Mauriello is an educator, author, consultant, and public speaker. He retired from federal service in 2012 after 30 years with the US Department of Defense (DoD). His assignments with DoD included special agent; chief of police; senior polygraph examiner; Director, Occupational Health, Environmental and Safety Services; Director, Interagency OPSEC Support Staff (IOSS); Deputy Director for Security Education, Training and Awareness; congressional staff investigator for the US Senate Permanent Subcommittee on Investigations; and Chief of Polygraph. He is a former police officer and criminal investigator.

He is the founder and CEO of the forensic consultant company, ForensIQ, Inc. His company provides forensic investigation services; criminal case and evidence assessments; security and counterintelligence services; education, training, awareness, and motivational public speaking presentations; and news media and film and TV production consultation.

His academic position as senior lecturer has been held concurrently throughout his professional career. It includes teaching criminal investigation and forensic sciences courses, while managing the Crime Laboratory for the University of Maryland at College Park, Department of Criminology and Criminal Justice.

He is an accomplished author, who besides writing this book, is the author of the legal treatise *Criminal Investigation Handbook: Strategy, Law and Science*; *The Dollhouse Murders*, illustrating crime scene dioramas used to study the crime scene investigation (CSI) process; and the e-textbook *Introduction to Criminalistics: From Crime Scene to Court Room*. He is the creator of the ForensIQ C.S.I. Checklist™ App, which is the first and currently the only mobile app of its kind that has been created to assist law enforcement and criminal investigation professionals while conducting crime scene investigations.

A sought-after forensic sciences consultant; he is regularly interviewed by newspaper, television, and radio news media. He has appeared on *ABC World News Tonight*, *CBS Sunday Morning News*, and Fox and MSNBC cable news shows. He has been featured as a forensic consultant on television documentaries, including The Discovery Channel's *Lizzie Borden Had An Ax*; and several episodes of Investigation Discovery (ID) Channel's series *Forensics: You Decide* and *Reasonable Doubt*. He is the creator and host of the TV webcast *ForensicWeek.com Show*, broadcast and archived on www. ForensicWeek.com.

His vast public speaking experience includes 42 years as a university professor; the presentation of hundreds of counterintelligence awareness briefings and forensic science lectures at numerous universities and law schools; as well as presenting his motivational seminar on public speaking communications titled "Motivation through Communication."

He is a recipient of the US Department of Defense, Distinguished Civilian Service Award; holds the degree of master of forensic sciences from George Washington University, Washington, D.C.; American Academy of Forensic Sciences (AAFS) Fellow; active member of the International Association for Identification (IAI), member of the Maryland Polygraph Association, Lifetime Member of the Operations Security (OPSEC) Professionals Society; and member of Maryland's Center for Forensic Excellence Advisory Committee.

Part I

General Preparation and Development

Chapters in Part I establish the building blocks to create your speech. Part I utilizes a communication model that illustrates each step that should be considered to satisfy the requirements for a successful presentation. It begins with meeting the presentation tasker who requested the presentation and moves on to create several short bulleted objectives that reflect the rationale for the presentation. It goes on to discuss different methods that can be used to transmit information from using audio/visual technology, to demonstration of hardware, to merely having the speaker verbally present information. The use of PowerPoint software is discussed to eliminate the phenomenon of "death by PowerPoint." Good and bad examples are provided to demonstrate the differences. The venue where the presentation is delivered in reference to the design of the space, its furniture layout, and audio/video equipment placement is also discussed.

Part I provides the reader with the essential elements for a well-planned and orchestrated oral presentation. If there is one image that should be kept clear in your mind after completing Part I, it is Figure P1.1 labeled "A Communication Model." With all the reflection tools presented throughout this book, this image represents the framework for creating any future speech or presentation you are asked to perform. It begins at the top left-hand corner, where it identifies the "tasker" discussed in detail in Chapter 1. Recognizing the needs and expectations of the tasker who asked you to present the topic in the first place will bring you straight

A COMMUNICATION MODEL

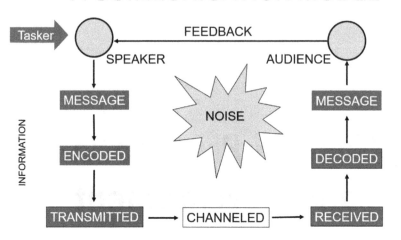

Figure P1.1 A communication model. (Created by T.P. Mauriello.)

down the model to identify what the "message" or objectives of your presentation will be, which is discussed in Chapter 2. Defining the proper message will prove to be the element that will guide you throughout the process. Not knowing the message for your presentation is what causes anxiety for you the speaker and lack of interest for the audience. The next step is knowing your audience, discussed in Chapter 3. These are the very people who are there to receive the information you have for them. Who are they, where did they come from, and what do they want to hear and walk away with are all discussed in this chapter. The audience will judge your presentation, so do not jump over this chapter; it is essential to your success as a speaker.

As you approach the bottom left-hand corner of the model, you will decide how you will transmit your information. Yes, this is an oral presentation, and yes, you will be talking, but what tools or resources do you want to use to get your verbal information "heard, understood, and remembered"? Chapter 4 discusses the various methods that exist today that can be used during the oral presentation. This can be accomplished by using PowerPoint slides, short video clips, live demonstrations, or just your voice and body language.

No matter what type of visuals you may choose, Chapter 5 will show you how to augment the spoken word with just the right amount of assistance from these technical marvels that tend to be overused at times. Whatever audiovisual equipment you select to transmit your message, this chapter discusses the need to prepare and test all the equipment to ensure it is in working order. The use of audiovisual equipment brings us to Chapter 6, which is the physical or virtual space you use to transmit to your audience the message they will receive. Being familiar and comfortable with the location of your presentation can reduce anxiety and allow you to reduce "noise," which is a term I use to represent roadblocks to effective communication.

Finally, the chapter that highlights Aristotle's principle that "It is not enough to know what to say; one must know how to say it."[1] Chapter 7 provides the ability to get your audience's attention, entertain them to keep that attention and eliminate the "noise"[2] that can distract your audience from hearing, understanding, and remembering your message. Referring to the communication model once again, you want to transmit information, have it received by the audience in the same manner as you transmitted it, and test the audience to ensure they have received what you transmitted.

NOTES

1. *Aristotle: Politics (Book 3).*
2. The term "noise" shown in the center of the communication model is defined by the author as any roadblock to effective communication, for example, not being able to be heard by the audience, sitting on uncomfortable seats, being too cold or too hot in the room, not being able to see the text on your slides, or not understanding terminology.

1

Meet the Tasker

INTRODUCTION

A communication model, illustrated in Figure P1.1, is used to view the entire preparation and development process. Chapter 1 begins the discussion by meeting the tasker. The *tasker* is the person or organization requesting you to deliver some sort of oral communication. Focusing on the tasker ensures that the speaker is clear about what is being required of them when asked to present a speech or give testimony. The speaker determines who the tasker is and obtains answers to the basic interrogative questions associated with the event. For example, why is the topic being presented? What are the objectives you want to attain? What questions can be expected to be asked by the attendees? Who is the audience? How many will attend? How much does the audience know about the topic already? What does the audience want to walk away with after the presentation? Obtaining this information will lead to a clear understanding of the "objectives and content development" for the presentation, which is presented in Chapter 2. The types of oral communications criminal justice taskers may request are listed with explanations for each.

When preparing for an oral presentation, especially in a public forum, you begin with meeting with the tasker. The tasker is the person who has requested the presentation, or it may be a requirement listed in a policy document from an organization's operational policy directive that contains clear objectives for you before you start. Either way, it is imperative that you have a clear understanding of the purpose for the presentation, the objectives you need to attain, together with the knowledge of who the audience is that will be receiving the information. More about the objectives and the audience

5

Figure 1.1 A meeting of the minds with the tasker. (From Shutterstock.)

later. Right now, let us focus on the living, breathing tasker. Too many speakers never bother to consider the importance of meeting with the tasker to learn firsthand what is being asked of them. Or, they get their instructions from a secondhand person who attempts to communicate to the speaker what the tasker wants and or tries to interpret what they believe they heard from the tasker to guide the speaker. This interpretation from the second person can become disastrous for the speaker and, at the very least, embarrassing. Don't let it happen to you.

STORYTELLING

I was the director of an interagency national security organization for the United States government. Shortly after the 9/11 terrorist attack, I was asked by the US Under Secretary of Defense to brief him on a specific program I was responsible for managing. He requested the briefing to one of his staff officers. His staff officer, in turn, forwarded the request to another staff officer from another organization in the hierarchy from which my organization was located. That staff officer became my tasker, but he wasn't my tasker, the Under Secretary of Defense was really my tasker. I violated my own rule by allowing the second staff officer to provide me with the objectives for the briefing. My staff and I spent two long weeks preparing for this briefing. On the day I presented it, I stood tall at the podium in the Pentagon feeling good about myself, my material, and what I was about to give. Yet, at the end of my briefing, what I heard from the under secretary was bone-chilling. He said to me, "nice job, but that wasn't what I asked for." I was left standing alone at the podium, feeling somewhat dejected, while in the back of the room were those two staff officers hiding their faces from me. I accept the blame for the failure to satisfy my one-person audience and his staff, and rightfully so. I had wanted to meet with the under secretary at the beginning of the process but was told by both staff officers that he was too busy. Now I wasted this busy man's time with a briefing that did not satisfy his needs.

THE TASKER

When you are fortunate enough to be able to meet with the tasker, make sure you are clear on what it is that you need from them. You need answers to the following questions in no particular order:

Question 1: Why do you want this oral presentation to be given?
   Is it to inform the audience?
   Is it to direct the audience to do something?
   Is it a mandatory requirement?
   Is it to change their behavior?
   Is it to influence their judgment?
   Is the presentation necessary, or is it just a nice thing to do?
   Is it to merely entertain, or is it to educate?
   Is it really necessary? Can it better be communicated in a written format, either with hard copy or electronically?

Question 2: What are the objectives for the presentation? (See Chapter 2.)

Question 3: What questions may be asked of you the speaker during the presentation or testimony? For example, when preparing your expert testimony in a court case, ask the tasker, who is usually the attorney for whom you are testifying, what questions might be asked of you from the opposing counsel. If your topic has content that may not be received positively by all in attendance, ask the

7

tasker what those issues might be and how can you prepare for them?

Question 4: Who is the audience, and why are they there? (See Chapter 3.) In the criminal justice adversarial environment, there are always two sides to the story with conflicting objectives. Make sure you understand all the issues.

This meeting with the tasker is vital to the success of your presentation. It will allow you to have a clear understanding of the topic, its significance to the audience, and how much content will be necessary. The results for you the speaker will be a feeling of confidence and being more relaxed on deliverance day. It is my firm belief that proper planning equates to an excellent presentation.

Let's not forget if you are working within the criminal and civil justice system, the taskers play an adversarial role and their objectives will conflict with each other.

Figure 1.2 Message regulated by policy. (From Shutterstock.)

THE TASKER BY POLICY

The other type of tasker is the documented policy or job performance requirement that goes with your job, for example, being assigned to the police–community relations division where your written job description lists the objectives required of you for each of your public speaking engagements in the community. In some cases, a written script for what to say may even be provided for you. Be careful when that happens; rigidly structured presentations that have been prepared for anyone to present can also be disastrous. Try to make the presentation your own, using your talent, skills, and personality. If you don't, your audience may not believe what you are saying when they see that you are just reading from a script. There are times when reading your speech is acceptable, but not in this situation. It has been my experience that organizational mission briefings that are usually presented when a visitor comes to an organization are given with no understanding by the briefer on who the visitor is and why they are there.

STORYTELLING

I was a senior manager who visited field sites throughout the world. Every place I traveled to, the protocol required that I sit through a mission brief ordered by the station chief. The mission briefing was an overview of the mission of the station I was visiting. I didn't understand most of the technical jargon being used by the briefer, and it never had anything to do with why I was there in the first place. Maybe, if the briefer used a language I understood, I may have benefited by it for general knowledge, but that never was the case. This is an example of a presentation that was not necessary to be delivered, but no one was willing to do anything about it.

My research in the field of public speaking has found that the importance of meeting with the tasker tends to be overlooked. Don't let that happen to you. Although your ultimate goal is to satisfy your audience, the tasker is the one who places you on the podium, and their needs must be met first. So, referring back to the communication model in Figure P1.1., you meet with the tasker to understand and create the objectives or develop the message. This will bring us to Chapter 2, "Objectives and Content Development."

THE TASKER WITH NO TASK

Figure 1.3   Confused. (From Shutterstock.)

Many times you are asked to be a guest speaker at an event. It may be a luncheon or dinner meeting, conference, high school or college class, training session, or town hall meeting. The person who invites you, the tasker, has no idea what topic they want you to present. When you ask them for ideas for your presentation, they respond by saying, "Anything, whatever you want, we are just happy to have you come and speak," or "Whatever you think will be interesting to the members." Many times what they are really saying is they are just glad they found you to fill the time slot. Don't let this happen to you. You will be the one standing at the podium before an unhappy audience if you haven't satisfied their interest. Many times the tasker has no idea what their role should be and that is why they are no help. They may not be experienced in knowing the importance of clarity for a guest speaker. What they are experienced in is being a member of an audience. So you may want to ask them to place themselves in the audience's shoes. Have them ask themselves, "What would you like to hear from this speaker?" If the tasker is no help or doesn't even exist, the speaker needs to rely on their ingenuity and decide for the tasker what they want. This is done by focusing on the audience's needs. Find out who the audience is and why they are attending the presentation. See Chapter 3, "The Audience," then you can develop your objectives and be on your way to a successful outcome.

CHAPTER REVIEW REFLECTION TOOLS

1. Use the communication model as a template for your speech.
2. Begin planning your speech by meeting with the tasker.
3. The tasker is the person who has requested the presentation, or it can be a written policy that lists the objects for you.

2

Objectives and Content Development

INTRODUCTION

Chapter 2 covers the development of your presentation objectives. The objectives agreed to by the tasker, discussed in Chapter 1, are the driving force that gives direction to the presenter about what content to include, how much time is necessary, and what methods to use when transmitting the presentation. Throughout the presentation development and delivery, the short bulleted written objectives become the governing tool from which all other content is derived. The presentation script development follows the content of the presentation. Chapter 2 discusses the three parts of a presentation – the introduction, the body, and the summary or conclusion – and the importance of ensuring that each is observable and measurable. The objectives discussion moves forward to the presentation outline that identifies specific subject matter in the presentation. The use of outlines, handouts, and other resource materials discussed provide the reader with all the tools necessary to have a clear plan. The concept of Mind Mapping is introduced in this chapter as a framework to create an outline.

THE OBJECTIVES

The established objectives for your presentation become the dashboard[1] for your content development. They are the bones that hold up the body of your presentation. They are the driving force that provides direction and content selection during the development process. When you have met the tasker or reviewed a policy document that lists the requirements for a standard presentation, you will be ready to determine the objects of your presentation. These objects are written as short, bulleted phrases that provide a global view of what your presentation is all about. There should only be approximately three to five of these bullets in an informative type of speech. Academic courses and training programs will have more,[2] but right now, let's focus on a typical speech or short oral presentation (Figure 2.1).

Figure 2.1 Listing objectives. (From Shutterstock.)

Do not be surprised if during the whole process of your content development that you want to adjust these objectives. This is normal as you explore the topic of your presentation and learn new information. Just be sure when you are making adjustments that you stay within the scope of the tasker's requirements. If you believe you need to go beyond those requirements, then go back to the tasker and have that discussion. Either way, before you begin developing the content of your presentation, make sure you are clear about the objectives and that you are comfortable with them.

There are multiple uses for the listed objectives. First, as discussed earlier, they are the dashboard to guide you through the entire process. Second, you will communicate these objectives to your audience at various times. For example, they can be part of an *abstract*[3] document you provide the audience ahead of time in preparation for attending the presentation. Finally, you will verbally present them at the beginning of your speech.

Because your audience is now aware of your speech objectives, those objectives must be *observable and measurable*. The audience needs to be able to recognize when you are discussing content related to each objective, and they need to recognize when you have completed that discussion and moved on to something else. In the event you do not get to one of the objections, don't apologize for it; never apologize for anything during the presentation. Why? Because the audience probably didn't even notice, and second, your audience does not want to hear excuses for your shortcomings in that regard. Speakers tend to apologize for things unnoticed by the audience, and when speakers do that, it brings attention to something that probably didn't matter in the first place.

The following are speech titles and examples of their objectives in a bulleted format:

Example 1 – "A Case of Double Jeopardy and How 3D Laser Scanning Clarified the Truth"

- Discuss an arson/murder case where the defendant was acquitted, but sent to prison anyway
- Explain why he was reincarcerated due to a parole revocation
- Speak about how a new forensic technology, 3D laser scanning, clarified the truth

Example 2 – "The Truth and Lies of the Polygraph"

- How to prepare for a polygraph examination
- How it works
- The polygraph interview and polygraph questions
- The polygraph as a process

Example 3 – "The Flipped Classroom: Turning Your Training Program Upside Down and Turning Traditional Education on Its Head"

- Examine the new pedagogy[4] movement
- Explain how this pertains to you (the audience)
- Consider these new options for your program
- Continue to "make a difference" by "making it different"

Example 4 – "Use of Small Unmanned Aircraft Systems (Drones) for Public Safety Operations"

- Define small unmanned aircraft system (sUAS)
- How they are used in law enforcement, security, fire, and rescue events

15

- FAA requirements for their use
- Examples of their use to date

Example 5 – "Critical Thinking: A Thought-Provoking Presentation"

- Clarify what we think we know, see, hear, understand and remember when communicating
- Introduce the 8 Elements of Thinking and 8 Intellectual Standards for Reasoning, which influence fact-finding, decision-making, and pursuit of the truth
- Present case studies that will have you rethinking the way you see the world

Example 6 – "Operations Security (OPSEC): Who, What, Where, When, Why, and How"

- Who is really responsible for it?
- What is it really?
- Where does it really belong?
- When does it need to be applied?
- Why should we care about it?
- How can we institutionalize it?

Example 7 – "Forensic Sciences, Evidence and Crime Scene Protocols"

- Forensic sciences – Defined, history, and application
- Scientific evidence standards (Frye doctrine and Daubert rule)
- Criminal investigation process and players
- Quality and usefulness of physical evidence
- Death investigation protocols

Example 8 – "Fingerprint Training"

- History and development of fingerprints
- Recognizing classification patterns
- Rolling and inking
- Digital Livescan technology
- Evaluating acceptable ten-finger print cards
- Familiarization of FBI Automated Fingerprint Identification System (AFIS)

Example 9 – "Your Attention Please! A Public Speaking Skills Workshop for Forensic Science Professionals"

- Focus on technique skills
- Being heard, understood, and remembered
- Customer-focused on the audience
- Facilitate thoughts and ideas for a useful, entertaining, and strategically planned presentation

Example 10 – "Introduction to Criminalistics: From Crime Scene to Court Room" (The following are the learning objectives from my e-textbook published by Great River Learning.[5] These objectives coincide with my lecture objectives in my Introduction to Criminalistics class.)

- Compare and contrast the study of criminalistics and the forensic sciences
- List the major disciplines associated with criminalistics and the forensic sciences
- Recognize the thought-provoking contributors responsible for the use of science in the examination of evidence
- Know the historical development of crime laboratories in the United States
- Understand the capabilities of forensic science and how it assists in solving a crime
- Compare Supreme Court decisions on the acceptability of the forensic sciences
- Explain the objectives of an investigation and the collection of evidence
- Recognize the pathway forward for the forensic sciences in the United States

THE OUTLINE

The *outline* is a one-page framework that highlights the main subject points that the speaker wants to cover. In simple terms, it puts the meat on the bones. It achieves three things for the speaker. It brings life to the objectives; it provides an overview plan to determine what content is necessary to satisfy the objectives; and finally, it can be used as s a handout for the audience to place the content in a logical order for better understanding.

Creating the outline can be the first barrier that a speaker experiences when preparing a speech. Trying to generate and organize ideas in an orderly fashion is not always easy. It requires the knowledge acquired from the tasker and a firm understanding of the objectives. You are halfway there if you are comfortable with these two processes. Traditional methods for creating outlines have trained us to do this in a linear fashion, beginning with idea 1, idea 2, idea 2a, and so on. Research has found that this is inconsistent with the way the brain functions. We understand and remember information by connecting one idea in our brain with another. In his book *Present Yourself*,[6] Michael J. Gelb states that all presentations are brain-based. For example, the presenter's brain "talks" to the brains of the audience members by way of creating ideas transmitted in the brain of the presenter and received by the brains of the audience. Ideas connect to create meaning, and the best way to achieve this is through a concept called Mind Mapping.[7]

> Mind Mapping was developed in the early 1970s by British author and brain researcher Tony Buzan. Buzan developed it as a whole-brain alternative to outlining. Mind Mapping makes it easier to access your ideas while enhancing your ability to organize them. It allows the analytical, detail-oriented left side of your brain to work harmoniously with the more imaginative right.[8]

A Mind Mapping Outline

Using Buzan's nonlinear Mind Mapping concept encourages you to generate ideas using keywords and images all on one page. The following steps guide you through creating a basic Mind Mapping outline onto a PowerPoint slide or paper:

1. Start your map with an image of your topic or the title of your speech in the center of your slide. This is your central ideas for your presentation. All other ideas will flow from this focal point.
2. Use keywords to represent subheadings flowing from your central image.
3. Connect the keywords with lines radiating from your central image.
4. Use colors, images, and codes for emphasis.

Figure 2.2 is an example of the Mind Map outline for my polygraph presentation that I have presented to hundreds of attendees in every kind of audience you can imagine:[9]

There are several benefits to using the Mind Mapping format to create your outline. The one-page document is to be used both as a slide at the beginning of your PowerPoint presentation and as a hard copy handout.

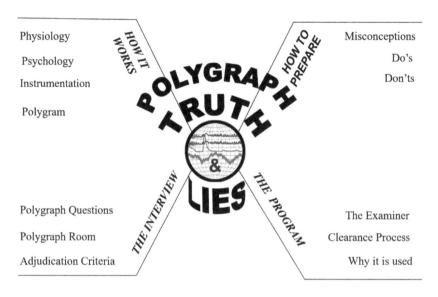

Figure 2.2 Example of a mind map outline. (Created by T.P. Mauriello.)

You are not held to a specific topic order, so you have total flexibility. The viewer is drawn to the center of your outline where the title of your presentation is located, and from there, the viewer can move around, up and down, and side to side to have their brain connect and comprehend the content. This particular presentation I have delivered to several different types of audiences with varying levels of knowledge about the topic and multiple needs and expectations. The Mind Map allows the speaker to jump around from subtopic to subtopic without confusing or distracting the audience. I most recently presented this very presentation to a group of criminal defense lawyers during a dinner meeting in which I was the keynote speaker. Because this was an educational event, what was important to present was anything that would satisfy their needs. I always tell my audiences that questions (Q&As) and comments are invited at any time. I'm not sure that invitation mattered, because the Q&As began immediately and never stopped. The good news was I was able to satisfy their needs and interests by moving around the Mind Map as their Q&As and comments brought me there. It was easy for me as the speaker and appeared logical to the audience using the Map Mapping format versus the more traditional linear format. We discuss further uses of Mind Mapping when developing PowerPoint slides in Chapter 4.

ORGANIZING YOUR PRESENTATION

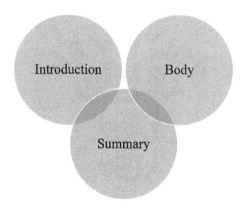

Figure 2.3 Three parts. (Created by T.P. Mauriello.)

Now that the objectives are clear in your mind and documented, let's begin organizing your presentation. There are three parts to any presentation. They are the introduction, body, and summary. "Tell 'Em What You're Going to Tell 'Em; Next, Tell 'Em; Next, Tell 'Em What You Told 'Em."[10] They are the same parts that we learned to create as children when we were learning to write a composition. A composition is a method a writer uses to assemble words and sentences to create a written communique. The word *composition* comes from Latin meaning "to put together." A speech is no different. The only difference is we are putting together words and sentences for oral communications rather than written communications. Notice that the preceding image has three equal circles for each of the parts. The message for you is that the development of each of the three parts is of equal value to the overall success of your presentation.

The Introduction

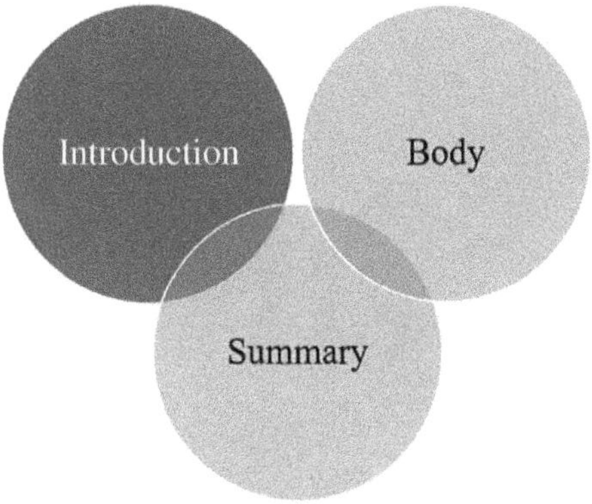

Figure 2.4 Introduction. (Created by T.P. Mauriello.)

"Tell 'Em What You're Going to Tell 'Em."

The *introduction* of the speech never gets the time and effort it deserves. Speakers tend to rush through any semblance of an introduction wanting to get right into the body of the presentation. The introduction is where you set the stage for the audience and establish the ground rules. This is where you are telling the audience what you are going to talk about; what the objectives are; who you are and why you are speaking on the topic; why the topic is important to them; what they should walk away with; what you expect of them in return; how long the presentation will last; when you will finish; whether you will be taking questions and if so when; and finally, if the presentation is over a certain timeframe, that you will be taking a break and when that will happen. No human being should be asked to sit and concentrate on anything for more than 60 to 75 minutes without a break. "The mind can absorb no more than the seat can endure"[11] (Figure 2.5).

Figure 2.5   Time for a break. (From Shutterstock.)

Introduction of the Speaker

Introducing the speaker occurs in several different ways. The preparation for the speaker introduction should begin before the day of the presentation. Whatever method of communication used to invite the audience, the same technique should be used to introduce the speaker as well as the topic and objectives of the presentation. Let's focus on the speaker right now. A short abstract identifying the topic and a biography of the speaker will suffice, identifying the speaker's name and organization. If your audience members are deciding if they want to attend this presentation based on what they see in the abstract, I suggest beefing up the abstract enough to give the potential attendees a clear picture of what to expect. For example, I have been presenting a workshop that on many occasions has been listed in the following manner: "Motivation through Communication," presented by Thomas P. Mauriello. That is the total information provided to the prospective attendees. Can you tell me what this presentation is about? I guess not. It isn't even the complete title for the presentation. The full title is "Motivation through Communication – A Briefing Skills Presentation." The subtitle at least provides you with a little more information. If the program manager/tasker for an event is trying to encourage attendees, they need to give enough information to entice the people to attend. Keep this in mind and don't be afraid to provide introductory text to the tasker. It will be appreciated.

Figure 2.6 Speaker introductions. (From Shutterstock.)

On the day of the presentation, a more formal introduction of the speaker should prevail, done by whoever is facilitating the event. The speaker needs to be appropriately introduced (Figure 2.6). If the facilitator asks you for your biography or asks you a few questions about your background to introduce you, give it to them. Don't be modest or think it is not necessary, because it is necessary. You want the audience to know who you are and what credentials you have as it relates to the subject you are presenting. The audience will decide how much of what you say they want to believe. The only way they can do that is to know your experience and knowledge about the subject.

On the other hand, if you don't have experience with the topic, don't share that with the audience. Don't lie to them either, but don't offer that up to them unless asked. If someone in the audience does ask you what your experience is, be honest with them and tell them you are new to the subject area but are excited about the opportunity to share what you know with them today. Remember, don't apologize for your lack of experience or anything else; the audience doesn't want to hear it.

So, what speaker introductory information is best for the audience to receive? It should be short but sufficient; enough for the audience to know who you are and why you are speaking on the topic. Here are some suggested bullets to have answers for when introducing a speaker:

- Speaker's formal name, title, and organization
- The expanded title of the presentation
- Why the topic is important and how it will make a difference

23

- The speaker's experience related to the topic (if any)
- Significant academic/training credentials as they relate to the topic*
- Significant honors/awards/accomplishments that relate to the speaker's credibility*

* For example, the audience does not need to know that the speaker was an Eagle Scout unless his topic is related to scouting or leadership activities. The same goes for awards or military medals. If these relate to the topic, it is fine to mention them; otherwise, don't waste valuable time.

Introduction of the Topic and Objectives

For the audience to benefit from your presentation, it needs to know at the beginning what to expect from the speaker. The speaker should make every attempt to make the presentation "personal," allowing attendees to feel that you are talking to them individually. It will motivate them to want to listen.

Do not rush the introduction portion of your presentation. You are building a foundation and creating a series of building blocks for the audience. The time you spend at the introduction will increase the strength of the body of the presentation and increase the value of the audience's understanding.

The Body

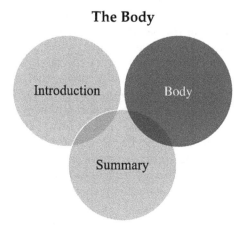

Figure 2.7 Body. (Created by T.P. Mauriello.)

"Next, Tell 'Em."

Now you are putting meat on the bones of your presentation. The *body* is where the textual content is presented that provides the evidence and facts of your case or presentation. The content in the body provides the supporting data needed to satisfy what is stated in the introduction. When you are creating the body of your presentation, you should always be referring to the stated objectives to ensure you are staying focused and not going beyond the topic area with information that is not necessary. When you write the first draft of a speech, it is common to have too much material in the body. This causes a loss of clarity and understanding for the audience and an inability for the audience to concentrate on what is being said. As you are rehearsing your speech, you will find yourself removing slides and information that are not necessary or don't support the speech objectives.

The Summary

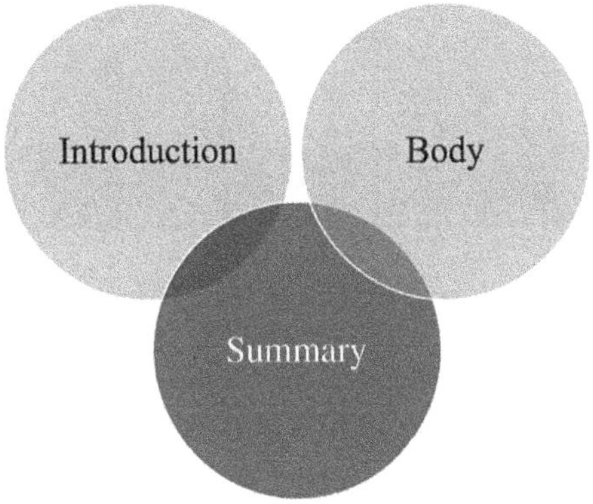

Figure 2.8 Summary. (Created by T.P. Mauriello.)

"Next, Tell 'Em What You Told 'Em."

The *summary* is the part of a presentation that gets omitted many times, especially when the speaker runs out of time. When the summary is omitted, attendees walk away with a lack of understanding, and their ability to remember valuable content is drastically decreased. Adults like repetition, and this is the time when the speaker can repeat and summarize the high points of the presentation and give the audience direction on what should happen, if anything, now that they experienced the content of the presentation. A perfect example of the importance of the summary is in a courtroom trial when an attorney is giving a summation to the jury. The attorney reiterates the high point of the case and the supporting evidence that proves those high points and then asks the jury to deliberate in their client's favor (Figure 2.9).

Figure 2.9 Lawyer's summary to the jury. (From Shutterstock.)

TIME MANAGEMENT

Time management must be considered when you begin writing your speech during the development stage. You have to consider how much time it will take to satisfy your objectives, complete all three parts of your presentation (the introduction, body, and summary), and leave time for questions and comments. It is difficult to judge how much time it will take to do all those things. You have no idea how many questions you may get from the audience if you are taking questions or allowing comments from the audience. At the same time, it is essential to stick to the time you have been given because your audience has mentally prepared themselves to concentrate only for that period of time. If you try to go one minute over, your audience stops listening. They start thinking about what they will be doing next in their own busy lives. Therefore, begin organizing your time right from the beginning (Figure 2.10).

Figure 2.10 Time to organize. (From Shutterstock.)

Another time management issue is when you are one of several speakers on a given day. It has been my experience that program facilitators do not do a good job scheduling speakers and breaks between speakers. For example, ten minutes is not enough time to conclude and thank one speaker, adjust audio/visual equipment, and introduce the next speaker. The result is speakers going over their allotted times, negatively effecting the entire program, and causing other speakers to have their times reduced. It is my opinion that going over your allotted time is disrespectful to both the audience and the other speakers, therefore be sensitive to time management throughout this process.

The only way to have some semblance of how long your presentation will be is to rehearse it. No speaker likes to do that (and I am one of those speakers), but you have to do that to determine if you have too much or not enough content or too many slides in your presentation. This is also a time when you should be deciding whether you will be taking questions from the audience. If your time is limited and you must finish what you need to say, then you need to consider not taking questions or comments. If you are going to do that, you must advise the audience of that at the beginning of your presentation, and tell them why, so they don't think you are ignoring them. You can suggest answering individual questions after the presentation is over at another time and location.

Figure 2.11 Watching the time. (From Shutterstock.)

Lastly, don't let your audience see you always looking at your watch (Figure 2.11). Many of us do this subconsciously, but when viewed by the audience during a speech, it gives the impression that you want to get out of there. When I am in control of the room in which I am speaking, like my classroom for example, I have a clock placed on the back wall. That way all I have to do is look up to see the time without drawing attention to it. Having your watch placed on the lectern is another way to pay attention to the time without it being a distraction to the audience.

Let time be your friend, not your enemy. Proper time management will reduce stress, increase your ability for success, and satisfy your audience. So, remember the six principles for time management:

1. Come early and begin on time. It reduces stress.
2. Gauge your time throughout the presentation to satisfy your objectives.
3. Be prepared to end on time. It shows respect for the audience and facilitator.
4. Stand up so you can be seen.
5. Speak up so you can be heard.
6. Shut up so you can be appreciated (Figure 2.12).

Figure 2.12 Time management appreciation by the audience. (From Shutterstock.)

CHAPTER REVIEW REFLECTION TOOLS

1. Objectives must be observable and measurable by the audience.
2. Don't apologize to the audience for anything. The audience doesn't want to hear excuses.
3. An outline highlights the main subject points that the speaker intends to cover.
4. A Mind Map is a one-page outline using keywords that represent the central ideas for a presentation.
5. There are three distinct parts to a speech: introduction, body, and summary.
6. Make your presentation "personal" to the audience. It will motivate them to listen.
7. The mind can absorb no more than the seat can endure. Give breaks.
8. Always introduce the speaker and the objectives of the presentation.
9. Do not go over your allotted time.

NOTES

1. The term *dashboard* is used here to identify a single document or slide that lists a series of bullets that allows you to visualize the performance indicators associated with your presentation. In simple terms it is a list of your objectives that can be referred to when developing content and your visuals.
2. See Chapter 10 in this volume.
3. An abstract is a summary statement of the contents of an oral presentation.
4. Pedagogy is the art and science of teaching and learning.
5. Thomas P. Mauriello, *Introduction to Criminalistics: From Crime Scene to Court Room,* "Module 1: Introduction, Learning Objections," Great River Learning, 2017, p. 1.
6. Michael J. Gelb, *Present Yourself,* Jalmar Press, 1988, pp. 2–3.
7. Tony Buzan, *The Mind Map Book: How to Use Radiant Thinking to Maximize Your Brain's Untapped Potential,* Plume, 1993.
8. Gelb, *Present Yourself,* p. 9.
9. The use of colors and images were removed to be compatible with the printing process of this book.
10. "Three Parts of a Sermon," *Northern Daily Mail* (*Hartlepool Northern Daily Mail*), August 13, 1908, p. 3, column 4, Durham, England (British Newspaper Archive).
11. Quote attributed to Morton Blackwell, president of the Leadership Institute, www.azquotes.com/quote/904150.

3

The Audience

INTRODUCTION

Chapter 3 focuses on knowing your audience. It is made clear in this chapter that the audience's attendance is the purpose of the presentation. Knowing who the audience is, where they come from, why they are there, how much they know about the topic, what they want to learn from the topic, and knowing when they are being satisfied are discussed in this chapter. Are they a mixed group of professionals, or do they all represent one particular profession? (See Figure 3.1.) How to recognize and deal with an adversarial audience in a courtroom, deposition, or town hall meeting; how and when to take breaks during a long presentation; and how to reduce unnecessary utterances, eliminate distractions, and create a comfortable environment for the audience in which to receive information are all discussed in this chapter.

PROFILING THE AUDIENCE

Figure 3.1   Audience profile. (From Shutterstock.)

Think and treat your audience as customers. When you do that, you start thinking of their needs and expectations right away. To be a successful speaker, you need to achieve that focus. Let us not forget that the only reason for us being asked to speak by a tasker is for the benefit of the audience. Whether you are referring to them as the audience, attendees, jury, triers of fact, senior leadership, management, the general public, or whatever else you want to call them, they should be the focus of attention for you the speaker. Here we will refer to them as the audience). As you talk with the tasker to learn the objectives of the presentation and begin creating the content for your speech, the knowledge and understanding of who your audience is will be essential for success. The questions about the audience that you should have answers for are as follows:

- Who are they?
- Where did they come from?
- Why are they here?
- What do they want to learn about the topic?
- How much do they already know about the topic?
- How many are there?

Who are they? You want to know as much about the audience as it is practical. If it is a town hall event, is it the topic of the presentation that has motivated the audience to be there? Are they potentially a hostile audience? If it is a conference or seminar, are they all members of a particular group or a general audience in attendance? Will there be media in the audience? The media usually has another motive for being there. Knowing the motive of the media will always be helpful.

Where did they come from? Are they local, or are they traveling a distance to attend? Is it a national or local group? Is it a mixed skill group with different needs?

Why are they here? Are they required to attend, or is it voluntary? Do they intend to be educated, trained, or made awareness of the topic? Are they expected to do something as a result of your presentation?

What do they want to learn about the topic? Is it consistent with what the tasker wants them to learn? If there is a conflict between the two, the speaker needs to clarify that long before the day of the presentation.

How much do they already know about the topic? Be careful here. You don't want to insult the audience by presenting information a majority of them already know, but you don't want to assume anything either. For example, if you are talking to a group of law enforcement officers about basic crime scene investigation and protection of evidence, find out what current training they have had since their initial police academy training. What you will probably find is they haven't had much training since then, and they do not know all they should know in regard to the topic. The tasker may not know the answer to this question either, so investigate this as best as you can.

How many are there? Why do you care about how many? There are several reasons to know the approximate number of attendees that will make up your audience (Figure 3.2). If you are distributing materials, you need to know how much to have on hand. I recently presented a series of five lectures on a cruise ship. I asked my tasker how many attendees I could expect at each lecture based on past experience. The answer I got was anywhere between 10 and 500. With that response, I decided to have anyone who wanted handouts from each of the lectures to email me, and I would send them a digital copy. I did have 25 hard copies for each presentation and had them available at the podium at the end of each presentation for those attendees who had a special interest in the topic. You want to know about the room you are going to use and if it is appropriate for the number of attendees. If you have some control over the location, then this information will help. But that doesn't always happen. For example, referring back to my presentations on the cruise ship, my first audience totaled 28-plus, and it was held in a skating rink arena that held 750 persons. My second, third, and forth presentations had between 75 and 100-plus attendees and were held in the main theater of the cruise ship that had over 1,000 seats. My point here is by knowing the number of attendees, you can try to adjust to create an environment that is most conducive to learning and comfortable for the audience. Encourage small groups of attendees in a room with a much larger capacity of seating to move to the front. Sometimes I actually use crime scene tape to section off seating and force attendees to move forward closer together. There is no need for "social distancing" among attendees as we are all forced to do during the coronavirus pandemic.

I have been adjunct teaching for over 42 years now, and I have been teaching the same course for 40 of them. Many of my friends, relatives, and colleagues ask me, aren't you tired of teaching the same thing over and over again. My response every time is no. No, because although it is the same course to the same type of criminal justice students, it is not the same students. The students are different every semester, and that is what

Figure 3.2   Half empty auditorium. (From Shutterstock.)

makes the course different every semester. It is the first time my new student audience is hearing the material, and that is what energizes me every time. Keep that in mind when you are giving the same presentation to a new audience. It may be old to you, but it is new to them.

ENGAGING THE AUDIENCE

Before you know it, you find yourself in front of the audience that you have been preparing for during the development phase of your presentation. The audience may be a happy crowd, an adversarial crowd, or maybe an indifferent crowd. What you do know is they are your crowd, and their focus is now on you. Positive interaction between the speaker and the audience throughout the presentation sets the tone for a successful event. You want the audience to like you, or at least respect you. You want to begin your presentation with confidence and a sense of authority. By authority, I mean that you demonstrate that you are in control, you have a plan, and you care about ensuring the audience is satisfied with the results (Figure 3.3).

You should never forget that the audience wants you to be successful. They are actually on your side, even during an adversarial setting like in a courtroom or town hall meeting, so don't look at them as the enemy. Why? Because they are all individually dying before your very eyes. Yes, every minute they spend listening to you, no matter what you are saying, is one less minute they are on earth. Whether they want to be at your presentation or not, they don't want to feel that they squandered their precious time listening to something that is a waste of their valuable life. Although that may be a little exaggerated, it is true. They are looking for an experience that will enrich their lives rather than squander it. If you have done your homework profiling the audience, then you should be prepared to satisfy their needs and expectations.

Something else that you need to be aware of is the 20/60/20 rule.[1] No matter how good your presentation is, 20% of your audience will not like you, 60% could go either way, and 20% will love you. Sorry, this is not just what research studies have shown, but in my 46-plus years of public speaking at all levels, it is what I have personally experienced. You see, it may not be you personally that they don't like; it could be your topic, or your organization, or the fact that they were forced to come to your presentation. How about the 12-person panel who weren't smart enough to get out of jury duty? How many of those people really want to hear your testimony in the courtroom? They were selected from

Figure 3.3 Engaging the audience. (From Shutterstock.)

their jurisdiction's voter registration database and by law are required to be there.

On one occasion, after teaching a four-hour workshop on public speaking skills, I received the student evaluation forms. One of the students criticized me for wearing a brown suit. They went on to say that brown was an evening color, and it was inappropriate for me to be wearing a brown suit during regular business hours. I reflected on what was meant for a moment, laughed, and then wondered what my parents had not told me during my formative years. So rather than focusing on what I was saying, this person was focused on my clothing. As a result of this feedback, I reflected on the 20/60/20 rule and simply placed this person in the 20% category of people who weren't going to like me anyway (Figure 3.4).

After writing the preceding story, I decided to do a little research on the whole idea of colors of clothing and if they had any effect on the speaker's

Figure 3.4 Selecting the right color clothing. (From Shutterstock.)

ability to engage their audience. I came across an article written by Alan Vinson in *The Business Journals* titled "Why the Color of Your Suit Matters."[2] Here is what I learned that applies to both men and women:

Navy – Navy is your power color. It connotes authority. You'll be perceived as a "take charge" type of person. Use navy suits for opening/closing arguments, public speaking, important presentations, and when you want to look like an expert.

Earth tones (including the color brown) – These are your "build rapport" colors. Wear earth tones to a staff meeting or team-building session, or when selecting a jury, delivering bad news, or meeting with clients and their families. Wear earth tones when you want to seem approachable. Keep in mind that people get the most compliments when they wear earth tones. So this is a reason why not to be concerned with what someone from the 20% group that doesn't particularly like you say about some aspect of your presence during a presentation.

Blue and gray – Blue and gray hues are your loyalty and dependability colors. They're great for traveling and are part of the "do everything" color family. Blue and gray are always appropriate. Those colors also convey a good work ethic. Wear blues and grays when you will be meeting with your boss or even your boss's boss.

Black – This is your most formal color. Use it in lieu of black tie or when you want to look cutting edge or fashionable. Like navy, black is also a power color. Wear black when you want to stack the deck in your favor. Think of black when you need to intimidate your competitor or want to outshine your competition.

Black and white – Black and white, as well as gray, are confident colors. Black and white combine to create a good suit for an average day. Nothing special going on – just a great look. They're also good colors that you can mix and look like you know how to dress.

Charcoal – Charcoal creates a rock-solid image. It shows that you are a pillar of the community and are trustworthy. Charcoal works well for professionals who work with finances, such as financial planners, bankers, CPAs (certified public accounts), and sales professionals. Wear charcoal, for example, when asking a jury for a big award, asking for a big sales order, and when asking for an investment.

Pay attention to what the audience is telling you as a group, both verbally or nonverbally. Ask yourself the question, "Are they paying attention?" One way to determine if your audience is paying attention and with you is to move around on the podium. Standing in one place too long can be mesmerizing for your audience. Being a trained forensic hypnotist myself, I am well aware of how easy it is for a person focused on one object, to fall into an altered state of consciousness. So leave the lectern and move around the podium in front of your audience.[3] As you do that, see if the audience follows you. If some of your audience is still looking at the lectern, you know you have a problem. In most cases, the individual attendees in the audience are probably "mind wandering," also referred to as "daydreaming," a natural phenomenon that research says happens during up to half of our waking hours.

> A unique human characteristic is our ability to mind wander – these are periods when our attention drifts away from the task-at-hand to focus on thoughts that are unrelated to the task … Research suggests that when we mind wander, our responses to information from the external world around us are disrupted. In other words, our brain's resources are shifted away from processing information from the external environment and redirected to our internal world, which allows us to mentally wander off to another time and place. Even though we pay less attention to the external world during mind wandering, our ability to detect unexpected events in our surrounding environment is preserved. This suggests that we are quite clever about what we ignore or pay attention to in the external environment, even when we mind wander.[4]

So the good news is it is natural for some of your audience not to be paying attention to you during your presentation. But it is not an excuse for the speaker to let it happen. It is the speaker's responsibility to keep the audience focused. That can be done by moving around the podium, as suggested earlier, raising the pitch of your voice, telling stories to support essential points, and asking questions of the audience. Figure 3.5 illustrates an advocate communicating with the jurors in a courtroom and having them all focus on what he is saying. Their nonverbal body language demonstrates that clearly for him. Part II goes into more detail on how to grab your audience's attention to help them hear you, understand you, and remember what you are communicating.

38

Figure 3.5 Jury – Getting your audience's attention. (From Shutterstock.)

ELIMINATING DISTRACTIONS – "NOISE"

Another responsibility of the speaker is to eliminate any distractions occurring while transmitting and the audience receiving information during a presentation. If you don't, the attendees annoyed by the distraction will transfer their annoyance to the speaker for not doing something about it. Referring back to the communications model (Figure P1.1), this "noise" as it is referred to,[5] can happen at any time during the presentation. It can be physical in nature like the audience sitting in uncomfortable chairs or sitting at tables that do not face the speaker, to being too hot or cold in the room, or loud noises coming from outside the room. It can also be audience members talking to each other while the speaker is talking, distracting those around them, or multiple attendees texting on their mobile devices. One way to deal with those people is for the speaker to move toward where they are and get as close as possible to them. While they are in the speaker's peripheral vision, wait until they see you standing there and stop whatever distracting activity they are doing. When you know that they are looking at you, simply walk away and allow your eyes to meet theirs for a split second. The nonverbal message is, "I see what you are doing and stop it right now." It usually works very well. You can do that to audience members who are sleeping. As their head is bobbing around and becomes a distraction for people within their sight, you move close to them until they can feel your presence. When their eyes open and look your way, do the same quick eye contact with them, and they will get the message (Figures 3.6 to 3.8).

A word about people sleeping in your audience: Don't misread their actions. Many speakers who are not confident about their speaking abilities tend to take this personal as if the person nodding off is bored with the speaker. That is not always the case. Most of the time, they are not asleep but in an altered state of consciousness. They actually can hear you, but because they are experiencing fatigue from a late-night event or they are suffering from a sleep disorder, they find it challenging to stay focused and to keep their eyes open. There are a lot of undiagnosed folks with sleep disorders out there.[6] I was one for many years.

When I was attending the police training academy at the beginning of my law enforcement career, one of the speakers reported me for sleeping during his block of instruction. The class would begin at 8:00 a.m., and I would be nodding off by 8:20 a.m. This was happening every day. I was not sleeping because as soon as the speaker announced a 10-minute break, I heard that clearly, and I was standing up ready to step outside of the classroom. I had been experiencing this throughout my high school and college classes. I didn't think anything of it then, but now it was getting me in trouble. It wasn't until I had several near-miss traffic accidents and my boss at work telling me it looked awful when I was sleeping during staff meetings that I sought help, and had both night and day sleep studies done. The result was that I was diagnosed with full-blown narcolepsy.[7] The good news is it is treatable with daily medication, and it is no longer a problem for me as long as I take my medication. Sleep apnea[8] is another common sleep disorder that is a condition related to breathing, where the airway becomes partially or fully obstructed during sleep. Sleep apnea is treated with a continuous positive airway pressure (CPAP) device used while the person is sleeping.

Whatever the reason for a person sleeping in your audience, if it becomes a distraction for others in the audience, you, the speaker, must do something about it as soon as possible. Certainly, don't embarrass the person in front of the group. Take a break and suggest to the person that maybe they

Figure 3.6   Audience sidebar discussion. (From Shutterstock.)

Figure 3.7   Sleeping. (From Shutterstock.)

Figure 3.8   Texting. (From Shutterstock.)

could sit or stand in the back of the room. Trust me. They will be appreciative that you brought it to their attention. The sidebar talkers should be handled similarly, except ask them to leave the room if they must be talking to each other. As far as the cell phone texting distractions are concerned, give clear instructions at the beginning of the presentation to turn off cell phone ringers and to be respectful of those around you not to distract them while engaging in unnecessary texting.

In a training or academic environment, the speaker has more control over the use of cell phones in the classroom. When my students come into my crime laboratory for class, they must place their cell phones in their team bucket for the entire time they are in lab class. My teaching assistant then secures them. I have justified this to the students by telling them that I care that they can hear, understand, and remember everything that is being communicated in class, and their cell phone is nothing but a distraction to that end. They have bought into this concept, and I have not had any pushback from anyone (Figure 3.9).

Figure 3.9 Cell phone depository during class. (Created by T.P. Mauriello.)

AUDIENCE DIVERSITY AND THE USE
OF SENSITIVE TERMINOLOGY

We not only live in a world that values equality, diversity, and inclusion of all people, their feelings, and way of life; we also expect to hear and see it in our daily lives. A public speaker must ensure that they are sensitive to all members of their audience and that their use of any words, images, or views, is all-inclusive and does not insult or offend anyone. The problem that exists for the public speaker is that it only takes one person to be insulted or offended to receive negative feedback. Although the negative connotation of a particular word, phrase, or image may be unintentional, it can cause a distraction that has negative results. Although a public speaker can't know and recognize the views of every audience member, the public speaker needs to understand terminology and images that are generally accepted and unaccepted by the demographics of their targeted audience.

What terminology is acceptable to the public changes from generation to generation, so the public speaker must keep up to date with cultural norms, and know their audience. For example, using the pronoun "they" rather than "he or she" is now the accepted way to refer to a person or group in general terms.

Groucho Marks (1905–1976), the American comedian, writer, stage, film, radio, and television star, was a master of quick wit, and widely considered one of America's greatest comedians. Groucho hosted a game show, *You Bet Your Life*, originally on radio in 1947 and then also aired on TV from 1950 to 1961. I recently viewed a number of his shows and although entertained by his humor, I was shocked to watch how he would communicate with the women contestants. His conversation with female contestants was filled with sexual innuendo and he was always referencing their looks, shape, and what they were wearing. On occasion he would ask the women for their measurements, and on two occasions he even asked two plus-sized females how much they weighed. By today's standards, these shows would be considered sexist, embarrassing for both the women on the show and the audience viewing it, and it would not be allowed to be aired today even on cable TV. But it was acceptable at the time. Audiences laughed, the contestants laughed, and everyone was having a good time. No one laughs at those sexist comments anymore, whether they are in a public or private forum. So be careful.

While I was writing this passage, it was reported in the news that the well-known cable news journalist and longtime host of the MSNBC show,

Chris Matthews, abruptly retired from his show, *Hardball*, apologizing for making inappropriate comments about women. He said that "compliments on a woman's appearance that some men, including me, might have incorrectly thought were OK were never OK. Not then, and certainly not today, and for making such comments in the past, I'm sorry." An interesting side note that has nothing to do with this subject but interesting none the less, when Matthews first arrived in Washington, D.C., he worked as a uniformed police officer with the United States Capitol Police.

I'm sure the baby boomers remember Elvis Presley's final appearance on the Ed Sullivan Show, January 6, 1957, when the TV cameraman was directed to only show him from the waist up while he was singing. At the time, it was believed to be offensive to allow the public to view Elvis' hip gyrations when singing, so the network censored it.

It has been my experience lately that some terms used to describe groups or actions have changed. For example, recently, while discussing a criminal case study with my class, I was describing the homicide victim in the case as a "transvestite," by definition, someone who adopts the dress, manner, or sexual role of the opposite sex. At the end of the lecture, one of the students in the class came up to me and said that she wished that I would stop using the word "transvestite" because it was an offensive term. I asked her what name she wanted me to use, and she stated, "cross dresser." Although one would argue both words mean the same thing, I have found it easier to use the term "cross dresser" when referring to a person who wears the clothing of the opposite sex. The term is actually more descriptive than the former term and doesn't even need an explanation when used. That leads one to the discussion of gender. I am not going there, but I did find a glossary of Equity, Diversity & Inclusion Glossary of Terms published by Pacific University, Oregon, and Diversity, Equity and Inclusion Terms published by the University of Houston for their students. I suggest reviewing these documents to ensure you use the most current terminology that is understood and accepted by today's audiences.

When creating slides that depict human subjects, always select images that represent the same diversity and inclusion as your audience. Your audience will respect you for that, and at the same time, you will eliminate any distractions that could have otherwise interfered with your presentation.

Some may remember when juries were not allowed to view crime scene photographs processed with color film. All photographs to be shown to juries had to be in black and white. The reasoning was that color images would inflame the jury and project a sense of violence beyond the act itself. As technology developed and black and white film went away, the justification for not letting juries view color photographs diminished.

In the event you are showing slides that are from actual crime scenes, be careful that no one in the audience has any connection to the subject matter in the images. I will never forget the time I showed a series of suicide crime scene slides from a local jurisdiction, and one of the students in the audience had a close relationship with the suicide victim. She was emotionally upset after the class and came up to me to tell me why. If I had known, I would not have used those slides. But how would I have known? Just be careful with sensitive subject matter, both orally and with illustrations. Of the hundreds of death investigation lectures I have presented to thousands of people, I only have had one audience member faint on me while viewing forensic pathology slides that required an ambulance response in the middle of the lecture. She was fine. She didn't require a transport to the hospital. She hadn't eaten for a while and was dehydrated. As soon as she was cared for, I was asked to go on and finish the lecture.

When selecting volunteers to participate in an experiment or other activity, plan ahead and ask those who are interested in volunteering to write their name on a sheet of paper and then pick the name of the volunteers out of a hat. That way, no one will ever suggest to you that you were favoring one group over another. I was always worrying about who to select without suggesting any favoritism. That is no longer a problem with the luck of the draw.

ELIMINATING UNNECESSARY UTTERANCES

The term *unnecessary utterances* refers to those filler words we tend to use to eliminate periods of silence when speaking. They are "ah," "er," "um," "you know," "all right," "so," "mmm," and others we use in our oral communication. It is a habit we all have, and while it is a natural habit, it requires attention here for discussion. Notice that the title of this section is "Eliminating *Unnecessary* Utterances." I have emphasized the word "unnecessary" because there is research that suggests that these utterances are not always a bad thing. Either way, their overuse can be a distraction that requires our attention.

Steven D. Cohen, a leading expert on persuasive communication and effective presentation skills, states that even though these words seem natural in everyday speech, they do not belong in formal presentations or speeches.[9] Cohen suggests rather than using one of these utterances, just pause, think, and then continue with your dialogue. This requires a lot of practice and persistence that I am not sure is worth the time and effort. Toastmasters International, the educational organization that teaches public speaking and leadership skills, includes an "Ah-Counter" during its club meetings. The Ah-Counter does just that. During each session, they count every "ah," "er," and unnecessary utterance that is made by everyone at the meeting. At the end of the meeting, the Ah-Counter stands up and report on how many unnecessary utterances were made and by whom. The idea is to help individual speakers recognize and reduce the use of these words during oral communications. It has been my experience that too much of anything going on during a speech can be too much, too many unnecessary utterances included.

Several years ago, I was presenting my public speaking skills seminar to a group of industrial security professionals. During the workshop, I discuss the use and misuse of unnecessary utterances. At the end of my four-hour seminar, one of the attendees came up to me and handed me a paper napkin with writing on it. That paper napkin is at the center of the slide shown in Figure 3.10.

I was shocked at first. I wasn't sure what his point was. Was he criticizing me? Was he trying to help me? I asked him to explain, and he said that he began to count how many times I was using the fillers. Not for any particular reason. He just did it. He told me I used those words as many times as you can see on the napkin. I thanked him for the information and told him I obviously needed to work on my use of these filler utterances. I had no idea I was doing that. It did demonstrate to me the need to consider this as a valid issue to be discussed.

Michael Erard, a linguist, consultant, and author of the book *Um … Slips, Stumbles, and Verbal Blunders, and What They Mean*, tells us "uh" and "um" and all the rest of them don't deserve to be removed from our speech. "There's no good reason to uproot them. People have been pausing and filling their pauses with a neutral vowel (or sometimes with an actual word) for as long as we've had language, which is about 100,000 years. If listeners are so naturally repelled by 'uhs' and 'ums,' you'd think those sounds would have been eliminated long before now."[10] He goes on to

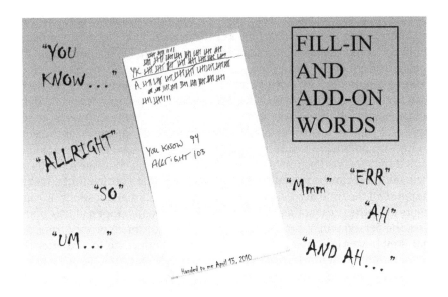

Figure 3.10 Napkin – Counting the speaker's use of unnecessary filler words during a seminar. (Created by T.P. Mauriello.)

say that the issue of eliminating umlessness didn't emerge as a cultural standard until the early 20th century in America when the use of the phonograph and radio became predominant in our society. Before this time, these fillers were unnoticed.

It is my opinion that beginners should concern these with other skills that need development and not worry about reducing or eliminating these questionably unnecessary utterances. The experienced speaker may want to work on them a little if they believe it is a distraction to their audiences. Either way, as I have stated over and over again, too much of anything is too much, so pay attention to your audience and determine for yourself if it is a problem.

HANDLING EXCESSIVE QUESTIONS AND COMMENTS

The speaker must be attentive to the individual audience attendee that is asking way too many questions or making way too many comments during the presentation. These folks are doing two things: first, using up valuable speaker time and, second, annoying the rest of the audience, because they are interrupting the speaker's flow of information. Don't let any one member of the audience take control of your presentation. Do not embarrass the person in front of the audience by asking them to stop asking questions or making comments. You don't want to prevent other members of the audience from engaging with you. Take a short break if necessary, and take the person aside. Tell the person how much you appreciate their interest in the topic and that their questions and comments are good ones. Continue by saying you only have a certain amount of time to present and you are concerned that you will be unable to finish on time if you continue to focus on their questions and comments. Suggest to them that you would be happy to spend all the time necessary to address any additional questions or comments after the presentation. Usually, two things will happen at this point. First, the person will apologize to you for taking too much of your time, not that they have to do that; and second, they will not come to you after the presentation. Trust me; they don't. It is as if they just wanted to be heard in front of the audience for some reason, and after you take that away, they are done.

INTERMISSION BREAKS DURING A PRESENTATION

Breaks are so crucial for both the speaker and the audience. It is hard for both groups to focus on a topic without a break. After 60 to 75 minutes, the brain needs a rest. Going beyond this time will cause the listeners to mind wander to the point of no return. Inexperienced program facilitators who schedule presentations tend not to be sensitive to this issue, so it is up to speakers to make this happen. It could be as simple as the speaker allowing the audience to stop listening, stand up for a few moments, and stretch a little. As previously stated, "The mind can absorb no more than the seat can endure."[11] Your audience will appreciate the opportunity to rest from receiving your transmitting of information.

Breaks in a presentation should also be announced at the beginning of a presentation. The audience needs to know if and when they will occur. That way if nature calls while you are speaking, they know how much time they have to wait for a break. If you don't tell them ahead of time, they will spend a great deal of time talking to themselves, thinking, "When is the break?" "Will there be a break?" "Should I just go now, or should I try to wait?" "I don't want to embarrass myself by getting up in

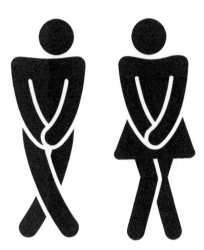

Figure 3.11 Time for a break please. (From Shutterstock.)

the middle of the presentation." "But I really have to go now." While the attendee is having this conversation with themself, they are obviously not paying attention to what the speaker is saying (Figure 3.11).

So for the audience's comfort, attention, and physical needs, *do not* go over 75 minutes without a break. Your audience will appreciate that you did.

CHAPTER REVIEW REFLECTION TOOLS

1. Treat your audience as a customer.
2. Begin with confidence and authority.
3. Be aware of the 20/60/20 rule: 20% will not like you, 60% could go either way, and 20% will love you.
4. Listen to what your audience says.
5. Watch what your audience does.
6. Your audience doesn't always receive what you transmit.
7. Your audience's mind constantly wanders away from what you are saying. Keep their attention.
8. Eliminate as much "noise" (distractions) as possible.
9. Pay attention to your use of filler words such as "ah," "er," "um," "you know," "all right," etc.

NOTES

1. See Scott Venezia, "Fact: 20% of Your Audience Will...," www.scottvenezia. com/fact-20-of-your-audience-will/; and Alf Rehn, "The 20/60/20/ Rule – Or Why You Shouldn't Worry about Frowns in the Audience," January 4, 2016, https://medium.com/the-art-of-keynoting/the-20-60-20-rule-or-why-you-shouldn-t-worry-about-frowns-in-the-audience-c9d31909a1e6.
2. Alan Vinson, "Why the Color of Your Suit Matters," *The Business Journals*, December 16, 2014, www.bizjournals.com/bizjournals/how-to/growth-strategies/2016/10/why-the-color-of-your-suit-matters.html.
3. You stand on a "podium" and stand behind a "lectern." A podium is anywhere a speaker is standing. It may be a stage, the floor in front of a stage, or the front of a classroom. A lectern is a piece of furniture or a portable stand on a table that a speaker stands behind that can hold a speaker's notes or laptop, and may also have a microphone attached to it.
4. Julia W.Y. Kam, "The Wandering Mind: How the Brain Allows Us to Mentally Wander Off to Another Time and Place," June 20, 2017, https://kids.frontiersin.org/article/10.3389/frym.2017.00025.
5. The term "noise" here is used to mean anything that distracts the audience.
6. There are an estimated 50 million to 70 million Americans affected by chronic sleep disorders that are undiagnosed or untreated. National Sleep Foundation, "Sleep Studies," 2019, www.sleepfoundation.org/articles/sleep-studies.
7. Narcolepsy is a neurological disorder that results in persistent, sometimes debilitating effects on sleep and daily life. People with narcolepsy frequently feel very sleepy and fatigued during the day, even after having a full night's sleep. Michael J. Breus, "Sleep Disorders and Your Health," https://thesleep-doctor.com/sleep-disorders-2/.
8. Ibid.
9. Steven D. Cohen, "Tips on Public Speaking: Eliminating the Dreaded 'Um'," Harvard Extension School, Division of Continuing Education, www.extension.harvard.edu/inside-extension/tips-public-speaking-eliminating-dreaded-um.
10. Michael Erard, "An Uh, Er, Um essay," *Slate*, July 26, 2011, https://slate.com/human-interest/2011/07/um-uh-ah-in-praise-of-verbal-stumbles.html.
11. Quote attributed to Morton Blackwell, president of the Leadership Institute, www.azquotes.com/quote/904150.

4

Methods for Transmitting Your Presentation Content

INTRODUCTION

Chapter 4 discusses the methodologies used to transmit information during a presentation. Included is the concept of always being *heard*, *understood*, and *remembered*. The first point made is that a presentation is oral communication. Therefore, there are situations that actually allow for and are best suited for the speaker solely standing before the audience with nothing but the sound of their voice and the nonverbal gestures of their body language. This chapter goes on to introduce the uses of audiovisual technologies such as PowerPoint slides and video clips, internet websites, live demonstrations, one-way communication lecturing, two-way communication discussion groups, question-and-answer periods, Mind Mapping, open forums, use of language translators, and the reading verbatim of a speech. Subsequent chapters will go into detail on how to integrate these methods into your presentation. The time allotted for a presentation, the number of attendees present, and the facility used to deliver the presentation, are all factors discussed in this chapter as a base to decide what methods should best be used to transmit content.

There is a presumption that when you are asked to give a presentation, speech, briefing, testimony, or any other oral communication, that someone believed it was important enough for the listeners to remember what was said. I learned this notion much later in my public speaking career, never recognizing the importance of the audience, remembering what the speaker had to say. We tend to be overly concerned about getting the information out, so having the audience remember what we say doesn't cross our mind sometimes. I knew it was important for the audience to hear you and understand you, but I hadn't included the idea of remembering. It wasn't until a friend and colleague of mine, Ray Semko, aka "The D*I*C*E Man,"[1] told me that some of the unorthodox techniques he uses helps his audiences pay attention and most importantly to remember what he was saying in his briefings. Early in his public speaking career, he got the impression that no matter what he was saying, his audience would leave the briefing room and had no motivation to remember anything he said. He believed he was wasting his time as well as his audience's time. We will be discussing several techniques Semko uses to turn that around, but right now, we will focus on the different methods for transmitting an oral presentation and how best to do that to help the audience hear, understand, and remember.

Edgar Dale, an American educator, who developed the "Cone of Experience," also known as the "Learning Pyramid," theorized through his research, that the least effective method for learning was just listening to the spoken words (see Figure 4.1). The most effective methods involve direct, purposeful learning experiences, such as hands-on interactive

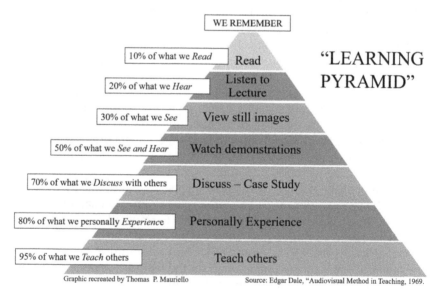

Figure 4.1 Learning pyramid. (Created by T.P. Mauriello.)

activities with the audience. This allows the audience to receive some authenticity to what a speaker is presenting.[2] Dr. Michael Hammer, in his book *Reengineering Revolution*, defined a lecture as "a one-way communication process, whereas the notes of the lecturer, become the notes of the listener, without passing through the minds of either one."[3] A little harsh but true. That is why today, traditional lecturing methods are slowly being replaced with interactive learning methods that have all the elements identified in Dale's Learning Pyramid.

PRESENTER ONLY

The following is considered TOP SECRET (TS) information that only those who have a "need-to-know" and have "special access" to this book can read. It must be protected at all times, and acting on its content may be considered unconventional and contrary to everything that you have been told in the past. Don't read it aloud in case there is someone in listening distance that is not authorized to receive it.

TOP SECRET

(TS) You do not have to use PowerPoint slides to deliver a speech, briefing, or any other oral communication. No kidding.

FOR OFFICIAL USE ONLY

Visual slides like those created with PowerPoint should only be used to augment the spoken word, not to be in place of it. If your topic is uncomplicated and time is short, you can prepare your presentation without any audio/visual support. Too many speakers are using too many slides as a crutch or as their content script. The audience shouldn't be viewing content slides projected on the screen for the speaker's benefit only. If you need an outline or script to keep you on track, then incorporate them in your notes placed in front of you or on your laptop that you only can view.

Luncheon or dinner speeches, keynote speeches, and welcome speeches at a meeting or conference all tend to lend themselves for "presenter only" presentations. Speaking without visual aids is certainly acceptable if the message is to inform, motivate, or entertain. Turning down the lights and turning on a projector isn't expected and can turn the focus away from the speaker. The audience should be focused on the speaker and what they are saying. When no slides are being used, there is nothing else for the audience to be focused on but the speaker, and that is the way it should be.

USING POWERPOINT SOFTWARE

How do we begin? There was a time before PowerPoint software was introduced when speakers wrote a detailed outline or script for their presentation and accompanied the script with a few selective viewgraphs[4] or 35mm slides. These slides were so expensive and time-consuming to produce, that slides were only used sparingly by speakers. They had to be created by graphic artists, and on many occasions, the speaker didn't have the time or budget to have them made. It wasn't until computer systems and quality video projectors became commonplace that the use of PowerPoint became popular and its use became widespread. Now slides can be produced by anyone. Here lies the problem. Now, when speakers are in the development stage of creating their speeches, they have replaced the script with PowerPoint text slides. So instead of the content script used as a guide for what to say verbally, the content script is on the slides for all to see at the same time. The result is the audience doesn't know whether to listen to the speaker or read the slides. This is why "death by PowerPoint" was born and has become rampant at all levels of oral communications.

The phrase "death by PowerPoint" is a phenomenon caused by speakers using PowerPoint software in a manner unintended by Microsoft®, or its original creator, Forethought, Inc.[5] The intent was to have speakers use the marvels of computer software programming to be able to create their slides quickly, eliminating the cost and time factor involved with creating 35mm slides and viewgraphs. PowerPoint slides were to help augment the spoken words, as did the 35mm slides and viewgraphs. What happened instead, speakers got lazy and decided to save time by creating slides to satisfy several other requirements. In addition to using PowerPoint slides as the content script, they are used in place of the presentation outline, handouts, and pre-briefing packages.[6] Slides should be used for what they were intended for – to augment the spoken word. They are not a teleprompter for what to say next. You can use PowerPoint to create all the other documents, but don't confuse them with your presentation slides. They are separate and distinct communications tools. The negative result is the slides have become information documents instead of presentation slides. Mostly everything that a speaker is going to say is now on their slides. The audience is either not listening to the speaker and trying to read their slides or not paying any attention to their slides. When they are trying to look at the slides, they are so dense with information that they have lost their effectiveness. The following Storyteller is a real example.

I was preparing to brief a group of senior leaders about a project and to accomplish that I was required to first present the briefing to his staff for approval. While I was giving the practice briefing to the staff, I made some briefing point and was immediately stopped by one of the staffers. They asked me if I was going to make that point during the actual briefing, and I said yes. They went on to say, "but I don't see that point on your slide." I responded by saying, "Yes, that is correct because I am going to say that verbally." They again went on to say, "But I don't see it on the slide." I again said, "But I am going to say it." They finally told me that I couldn't make the point verbally without it being on the slide. I told them that it was absurd, and began giving them my lecture on the proper use of PowerPoint slides. They looked at me as if they were hearing it for the first time. I asked them where it was documented that I had to have everything I said on my slides, and at that point, they stopped talking. I didn't make friends that day, but I didn't need any more friends at that point in my life.

If a speaker attempts to place everything they want to say on their slides, two things will happen. First, the benefit of the slides as a tool to augment the spoken word will be lost and, second, the slides will no longer be slides but a series of documents that can be printed out and read by the audience at their leisure. You might as well cancel the oral presentation. The preceding example is not an isolated event. It often happens in the professional world. My only recommendation in this regard is if you are forced to provide a lot of factual data prior, during, and after your presentation, and you are going to use PowerPoint to create this information, then create a hardcopy of the PowerPoint slides for the audience as a handout and create a separate PowerPoint presentation with slides that you will use exclusively for your oral presentation.

Presentation Slides

When you are constructing slides for linear use, meaning one slide after the other, try to stick to the 6/30 rule. That is 6 slides per 30 minutes of oral presentation. That number will increase for certain types of presentations like a scientific presentation where statistics and other tables and research data needs to be presented. But in an informative type of speech, the 6/30 rule should prevail.

When choosing a font for your presentation, you want to make sure you use a font that will be supported by any computer that is opening your presentation. It is interesting to learn that the default font for PowerPoint is Calibri, which is not one of those. Several fonts are 100% safe to use with all versions of PowerPoint with a PC or Mac.[7] Those fonts are

Arial	**Arial Black**	Comic Sans
Courier New	**Impact**	Georgia
Times New Roman	Trebuchet MS	Verdana

You want to choose a *font* that is easy on the eyes and easy to read. I have always used Times New Roman as my first choice, and sometimes I will use Arial. Either one is my recommendation. The only time I will use other fonts besides the primary font I am using is when a particular slide has a specific type theme that I am trying to emphasize, and I find a font that supports that theme.

Font size is the next important consideration to think about for your audience's readability. Don't use a font any smaller than 18 point and preferably use a 24 point as the minimum size. The larger, the better as long as there is a balance between your text and any image that accompanies it. See Figure 4.2 for an example. Before my audience comes into the room where I will be presenting, I project several of my slides onto the projection screen and then go to the farthest point from the screen to make sure the slides are readable. No matter how large the room or auditorium has been, the aforementioned font sizes have been more than adequate. There is nothing worse than hearing a speaker apologize to the audience for the text on their slides being too small to read. It is a poor showing for two reasons. First, it is simple to change font size and not doing that shows a total disregard for the audience. Second, never apologize to your

40 pt. **ACE-V Process for Latent Print Identification**

36 pt. **A**nalysis – quality of the print
Comparison – class characteristics
Evaluation – individual characteristics
Verification – quality control process

Figure 4.2   Example of Arial font. (Created by T.P. Mauriello.)

audience. They don't want to hear apologies or excuses for not doing something. Sometimes you listen to speakers apologizing for things the audience didn't even know were happening or not happening. Now the speaker has brought it to the audience's attention, and that is never good.

Font colors are the next consideration. The only thing I will say about font color is that a dark color font against a dark color background cannot be seen clearly; the same thing for a light color font against a white background. You cannot see them, so stay away from those combinations. I am not an artist like my wife who tells me my slides are sometimes too busy,[8] so I am not going to discuss artistic considerations of blending colors with certain images, etc.

Whether you are considering font color, slide background colors, or colors associated with illustrations or images in your slides, there is some research on color choices in this regard and how certain colors affect the audience attention. Noah Zandan, the CEO and co-founder of Quantified Communications, is pioneering the application of science and data to identify how people and especially leaders and public speakers communicate. In his article, "Color Psychology – What Colors Make Great Presentations?" he lists the following colors and how they affect the audience's attention and decision making:[9]

- Red stimulates attention to detail – along with excitement, as noted earlier – because people associate the color with danger, making them more cautious.

- Blue encourages creativity because it is associated with a peaceful environment in which it's safe to explore. This color is also associated with conservativism and tranquility, which is why it's often used in the corporate world.
- Green is perceived as warm and emotive, and encourages discussion and interaction.
- Yellow is an attention-grabbing color, great for highlighting key points. It's also been found to stimulate mental activity and enhance memory.
- Purple, a color once associated with royalty and rarely found in nature, is considered exotic and luxurious and fosters creativity.

The *6×6 Presentation Rule* suggests that you should have no more than six words per line and no more than six bullet points per slide. The goal is to keep your slide from being cluttered with so much text that your audience doesn't want to look at it. The 6x6 Rule isn't a steadfast rule; it is just a gauge for you not to overdo it. I have a gauge to ensure that my slides augment what I am saying without replacing what I am saying. The indicator is this: If the slide can stand alone and the viewer can receive the total message, then it is not a slide, it is a document and Word should have been used rather than PowerPoint. Your slides should act as a framework for your key points. They should allow the viewer to frame your idea so you can then fill in the facts. The following is a before and after example of a pair of text slides, Figure 4.3 and Figure 4.4, that demonstrates a slide with too much text that could stand alone without the need for a presenter, and then the same slide recreated with less text and short bullets that frame the topic for the presenter to fill in the information verbally:

Busy slides are those that generally have too many things going on in them. It is impossible to read the text, and there is no focus on one particular image, so the viewer doesn't know where to look. They are usually recommended not to be used, but under certain conditions, they may make an important point for the speaker. For example, Figure 4.5 is a very busy slide that contains a lot of data. It is an image of a bank accounts accounting finance forensics spreadsheet with magnifying glass and pen. If you were presenting a lecture on financial forensics and wanted to give the audience an appreciation for one of the tools that represent the concept for financial fraud investigation, audit, and analysis, a PowerPoint slide made from Figure 4.5 would make that point. You would not be asking the audience to try to read the data or you would not be directing their attention to any of the data for comprehension. You are just supplementing what

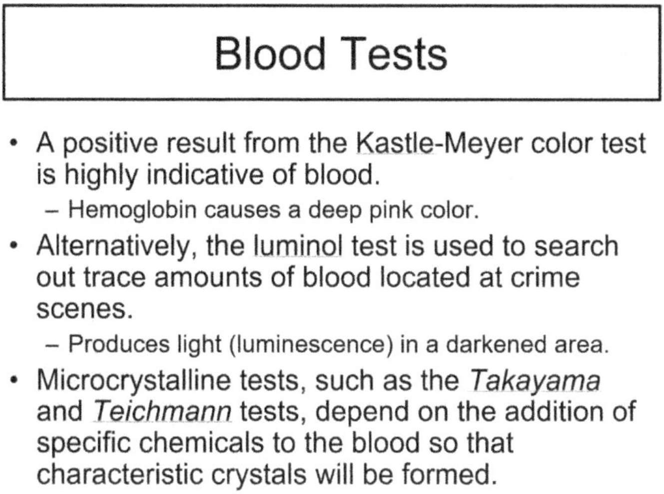

Blood Tests

- A positive result from the Kastle-Meyer color test is highly indicative of blood.
  - Hemoglobin causes a deep pink color.
- Alternatively, the luminol test is used to search out trace amounts of blood located at crime scenes.
  - Produces light (luminescence) in a darkened area.
- Microcrystalline tests, such as the *Takayama* and *Teichmann* tests, depend on the addition of specific chemicals to the blood so that characteristic crystals will be formed.

Figure 4.3   Before text slide example. (Created by T.P. Mauriello.)

Blood Tests

- Kastle-Meyer color test
  - Hemoglobin causes a deep pink color.

- Luminol test
  - Produces light (luminescence) in a darkened area.

- Microcrystalline tests
  - *Takayama* and *Teichmann*
  - Characteristic crystals are formed.

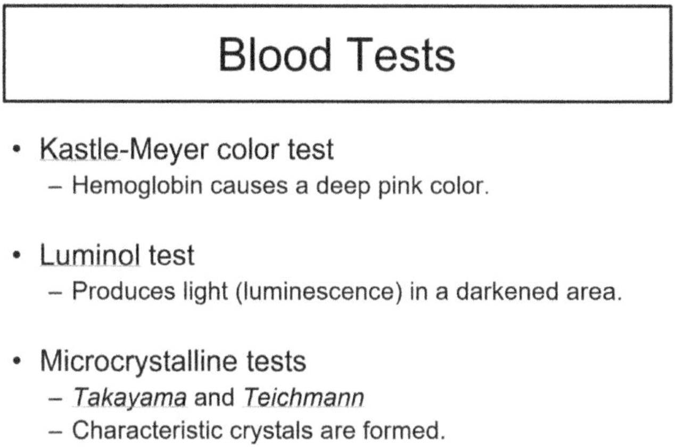

Figure 4.4   After text slide example with same content message as Figure 4.3. (Created by T.P. Mauriello.)

you are verbally stating with an image that provides the audience with a visual that helps the audience understand.

The use of PowerPoint and how to create slides is a subject in itself. The internet is full of books, articles, ideas, suggestions, and programs on how to best use PowerPoint. I have used Dr. Cliff Atkinson's book *Beyond*

Figure 4.5 Example of an acceptable busy PowerPoint slide. (From Shutterstock.)

Bullet Points as an excellent reference to gain additional skills in its use.[10] For right now, remember the following when using PowerPoint or any other similar program:

- Don't read your slides during the presentation. (They should not be your notes.)
- Consider the 6×6 Rule. (See earlier. Limit the amount of text and number of bullets in each slide.)
- Don't turn your back to the audience to view your slides. (Have your laptop in front of you so you can face the audience and still view your slides.)[11]
- Stand close to the projection screen while presenting, so the audience can quickly move their eyes from you, the speaker, to the slide, and then back to you, the speaker. (See Figure 4.6.)
- Don't overuse standard PowerPoint clipart. (Audiences are tired of seeing the same stick figures over and over again.)
- Eliminate text-heavy slides. (Remember, if the text in the slide can stand alone for the message to be understood, it is not a slide, it is a document.)

Figure 4.6 Speaker standing next to the projection screen. (From Shutterstock.)

- Make sure the font used can be viewed comfortably from the back of the room. (24 point is best; 18 point minimum if necessary.)
- Transitions shift from one slide to the next.[12] (Select one type of transition and stay with it throughout the presentation.)
- Never trust your audiovisual technology. (Test your equipment and the software you will be using in the facility where you will be presenting.)
- Limit the use of sound effects embedded in your slides. (Too much of anything is too much.)
- Use good color contrast. (With fonts and slide backgrounds.)
- If the slide doesn't augment what you are saying, delete it from the presentation. (It is not needed.)
- No need for slides. (A possibility in some cases.)

Mind Mapping and Use of Hyperlinks

We discussed in Chapter 2 using Mind Mapping[13] as a tool to create a one-page presentation outline. Now let's talk about the real significance of using Mind Mapping to create a PowerPoint slide presentation. Mind Mapping allows the speaker a method to present information that is consistent with the way the brain functions, learns, understands, and remembers. In its simplest terms, it does that through association. It is associating one idea or concept with another. So what we want to do for the audience is spread the keywords that represent the key topics of a presentation in front of the eyes of the audience on one slide. From there, we can branch off to subkey topics created on other slides, always connecting back to the original slide. The traditional method of presenting slides linearly, one after another, is inconsistent with the way the brain works. For example, have you ever been listening to a presentation where the speaker refers to a previous slide or previous information that is no longer on the screen? You find yourself wanting to ask the speaker to bring that slide back up, or the speaker attempts to do that themself, which can be a difficult thing to do. With a Mind Mapping slide, that is not a problem. Following is an example of my recent Mind-Mapped slide presentations. It is a presentation that I have given numerous times to numerous types of audiences.

This Mind Map slide represents a 1-hour presentation that can be reduced to 30 minutes or increased to over 2 hours. One of the benefits of using Mind Mapping slides versus linear aligned slides is the flexibility of moving from one subtopic to another subtopic. The focus of the presentation is in the middle, "The Truth and Lies of the Polygraph." I have broken down that main topic into four distinct subtopics: "How to Prepare," How it Works," "The Interview," and "The Program." Each one of those sub-topics continues to be reduced to additionally connected subtopics. All these key topics are seen together on one single Mind Mapping slide, as shown in Figure 4.7. Each of the keywords on the slide is a hyperlink[14] to another group of slides or other media. The Mind Map you see in Figure 4.7 actually has 72 PowerPoint slides, 5 video clips, 1 video show, and 1 pamphlet document included in the single PowerPoint file. The audience doesn't know that. They only see and hear what you present to them. Because you can jump around from one subtopic to another, you have total flexibility to focus on the needs and expectations of your audience. I mentioned that I had presented this presentation several times to several different audiences. I have given it to criminal justice students in an academic environment, contractors in a professional setting who were preparing to take a polygraph for a clearance or employment, and most recently I presented it at a dinner meeting for a criminal defense attorneys association, who had all levels of knowledge about the topic. They all had different interests and needs, and by using the single Mind Mapped PowerPoint presentation, I was able to satisfy their needs as if it was prepared just for them.

Figure 4.8 is an example of how to create a hyperlink. You highlight a word, icon, or image that you want to hyperlink from on the slide.

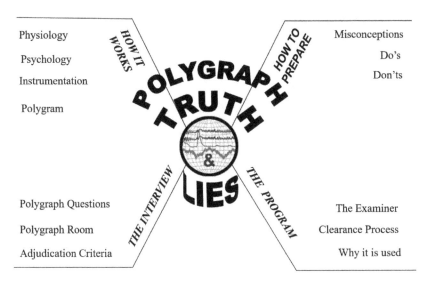

Figure 4.7 Example of a PowerPoint-created mindmapping slide. (Created by T.P. Mauriello.)

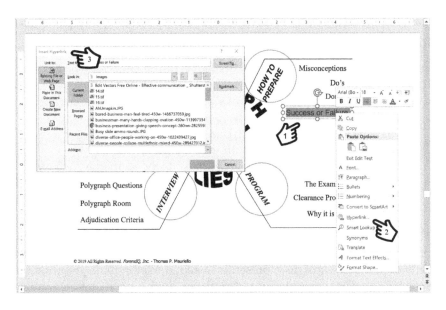

Figure 4.8 Example of PowerPoint Hyperlink windows. (Created by T.P. Mauriello.)

(See click 1.) Then click on the word Hyperlink... (See click 2.) Finally, the Insert Hyperlink window pops up. (See click 3.) It is in this window that you decide where you want to hyperlink to.

VIDEO CLIPS

Embedding short video clips into your PowerPoint presentation can make enormous positive impressions with your audience. They should be no more than 30 seconds to 5 to 7 minutes in length. With today's technology, there is no excuse for not considering its use. Your smartphone takes high-quality video where you can produce short video clips or, of course, you can download YouTube video clips.[15] Embedded video does several things for the speaker and your presentation to add a positive experience for the audience:

- It grabs their attention. (It brings the audience back from mind wandering.)
- It expands their visual view beyond the walls of the venue. (You allow the audience to see something besides you the speaker on the podium.)
- It provides clarity to complicated concepts. (This is especially beneficial when speaking to non-science or non-legal professional groups.)
- It is entertaining. (If you are not entertaining your audience, they are not listening to you.)
- It provides a different point of view. (Beyond that of the speaker.)
- It offers additional content. (Beyond the knowledge of the speaker.)
- It can be a great icebreaker.[16] (Used at the very beginning of a presentation to build rapport with the audience.)
- It can balance the use of time. (Using blended media increases learning.)
- It can introduce comments from other experts in the field. (This can give credibility to the presentation.)

The term *embed* the video into your PowerPoint presentation means a simple click of a hyperlink in a slide will begin the video. In the past, unfortunately for some still now, presenters needed to stop their presentation, switch to another computer or video player, double-click on it, maximize the video, adjust the sound (hopefully it works), move the mouse cursor out of the way, play the video, and then reverse engineer what was done to get back to their slides. It kills the flow of the presentation and gives the appearance that the speaker needs to apologize. Remember, never apologize for anything. Just keep moving on. Embedding videos is the way to go, and if you don't know how to do that, ask a young person to help you. They probably have been using PowerPoint longer than you have.

The copyright issue for using video clips is very confusing. I have sought consultation from federal government copyright attorneys, and they never agree to where the line is drawn. I suggest consulting with your attorney when using videos, slides, images, photographs, or any other media that was created by someone else. Even if you are not receiving compensation for delivering a speech, you still need to abide by copyright laws.[17]

INTERNET

In the same manner, when you can hyperlink from a slide to a YouTube video on the internet, you can also hyperlink from a slide to any internet uniform resource locator (URL). A URL is simply the internet address for a website. All you are doing is going from the slide to the internet, so whatever URL you go to, it is not embedded in your PowerPoint presentation. Therefore, if you want to use this internet hyperlink, you will have to be connected to the network at the venue where you are speaking. Obtaining internet access is getting easier and cheaper, even free, every day. In the more recent past, convention halls and hotels charged enormous fees for internet access in their spaces, but this is slowly changing, and I am finding that those fees are going away. Either way, you must find out from your tasker whether internet access will be available for you. If there is internet available, you may also want to ask if there is a fee and who will be paying for it. I didn't do that one time, and the tasker tried to get me to pay a $600 fee for two hours' worth of internet access at a convention center venue. Don't worry, that was a while ago, the year 2014, and no, I didn't pay it.

LIVE DEMONSTRATIONS

Referring back to Edgar Dale's Learning Pyramid (Figure 4.1), we are reminded that when we can both "see and hear" information being presented to us, the ability to understand and remember, is increased to 50%.

Live demonstrations require a lot of preparation and thought. It includes going back to your tasker to determine if performing a live demo is worth the time and effort it takes. Questions to be asked are: How much extra time will it take to prepare the audience to understand the demonstration? Is the demonstration necessary? Will all the audience be able to see the demonstration while it is being performed? What percentage of time will be taken away from the main content of the presentation? Does the demonstration have a direct link to the presentation objectives? Will the audience be disappointed if there is no demonstration? What items and equipment will have to be brought to the venue to conduct the demonstration? Is the presentation of an academic or informative learning experience or training for the audience? Will the audience be expected to perform a skill or activity represented in the demonstration? Answers to all these questions are necessary before a decision is made to conduct a live demonstration of any type.

For example, I am a trained forensic hypnotist and frequently present an informative talk on forensic hypnosis. When I give it as an academic lecture with unlimited time to use, I always conduct a live demonstration by asking for volunteers and hypnotizing a group of approximately six to eight persons from the student audience. The demonstration takes a minimum of 75 minutes to complete. It requires identifying student volunteers who want to experience being hypnotized. The signing of waiver forms ensure the volunteers don't hold the university libel for any unforeseen reason. Inducing them into hypnosis and having them experience something that illustrates to both the student subjects and the student audience that they are really experiencing hypnosis. And finally, taking them out of the altered state of consciousness that they were in and having them discuss with the audience what they felt throughout the procedure. Figure 4.9 is a photograph of one of those demonstrations conducted in a lecture hall at a university.

Most times, when I am asked to talk on forensic hypnosis, the maximum time I have is one hour, and that is not enough time to do any demonstration. The audience understands that and appreciates the detailed discussion on the subject. There are times when the live demonstration can be a show-and-tell. My best example for this type of demonstration is when conducting my firearms identification and awareness lecture with my long-time friend, colleague, and guest lecturer expert Robert "Beau" Moulden. The objective of this lecture is to give my students, the future law enforcement officers and criminal lawyers of the world, an appreciation for all types of weapons and an understanding of the forensic value

Figure 4.9   Forensic hypnosis demonstration conducted by Professor Mauriello.

for each category of weapon seen on the streets today. The students get to view, handle, open, and ask questions on every type of weapon you see displayed in Figure 4.10. So in this type of live demonstration, the activity is integrated with the lecture. There is no timing issue. Just the time for my guest to pack up all his weapons from home, bring them to the university, unpack, and pack them up again to return home.

LECTURING

There was a time when I would tell you that the one thing I loved most about teaching was lecturing to large lecture halls of students. The bigger, the better. I was able to engage students, watch them follow me as I moved across the podium and up and down the aisles. I was able to effectively prompt students to interact with me and other students, asking questions, making comments, agreeing, and disagreeing with what was being said. I did that 3 hours a night, 2 nights a week, for over 30 years. Then it slowly began to stop. It became difficult to engage students like before. They were not asking questions and making comments anymore.

Figure 4.10 Firearms demo.

They would go home from my lecture and send me an email or text message asking me a question about the lecture material I presented to them earlier that same evening. They now wanted a personal response from me rather than asking it during the class and letting everyone hear the answer. It got to a point where I was the only one talking. I became concerned that maybe Dr. Hammer was right when he defined a lecture as "a one-way communication process, whereas the notes of the lecturer, become the notes of the listener, without passing through the minds of either one."[18] It was evident that technology had changed the way people wanted to learn.

Today's generation would much rather get information using the technologies they have been brought up with. They also want to get that information at their own pace and when they feel like getting it. That's when I left the lecture hall and transformed my courses into a blended learning format. We will discuss this later in Chapter 10, but right now, let's get back to the one-way communication lecture format. Let me make it clear here. I still love lecturing in the same way I have done in the past. My message here is, it's going away, classrooms as we knew them are going away, the way we learn is changing, and those who teach and speak in public are not keeping up.

We still have a large lecture hall, and some even still have chalkboards in them. The problem is that many lecturers are not paying attention to their students and what they are doing in their seats. The students are on their cell phones texting and surfing the web on their laptops. They are not listening the way they had to before technology gave them much of their information via electronic textbooks and learning management systems (LMS).[19]

In regular public speaking presentations, we still find the one-way lecture format still prevalent. We call it something else. We call it a speech, a talk, a plenary session,[20] or a keynote address. These have more value because they are not presented in an academic setting. My recommendations for those who are giving these types of presentations are to use slides to augment what you are saying, move away from the lectern, and get down to the floor level with your audience when you logistically can do that. You will give the audience a feeling that you are engaging them and care about their presence in the audience.

READING A PRESENTATION VERBATIM

It would be easy to suggest that you should never read your speech, but reality says otherwise. There are occasions when you have to read a speech verbatim because one of the following reasons has presented itself.
When you must read a speech:

- Someone else has written an address that you have been asked to deliver.
- Circumstances of unavoidable events have placed constraints on your time for the usual preparation.
- You are asked to deliver a speech at the last minute. For example, the night of the viewing of a friend at the funeral home, a family member asks you to deliver the eulogy for them.
- A formal occasion, when you have to choose your words carefully.
- You are not familiar with the topic.
- Emotional speech – wedding or eulogy.
- A lawyer requires you to read a statement word-for-word.
- Giving testimony before the United States Congress.
- Reading a passage from another work.

Problems reading a speech:

- Your eyes are mostly looking down at the page, and you are not connecting with the audience. You lose that personal touch with the audience.
- Your head is slanted downward, which inhibits your vocal projection.
- Reading text loses that conversational style of delivery.
- Your vocal variety tends to be limited.

Now that we have discussed all the negative reasons and occasions for reading a speech, let's discuss how to get through delivering one as best as you can. Like any speech, you need to have a plan, and you will need to do some rehearsing. We start by creating the written script.

Preparing the written script (see Figure 4.11):

- Write as you talk – you will be more believable that way.
- Type it out – don't handwrite it. You don't want to have any trouble being able to read your handwriting.

Figure 4.11 Reading script template. (Created by T.P. Mauriello.)

- Use two columns rather than typing across the entire page. That way, the audience will not watch your head moving back and forth from one line to the next. You can find the column tab in the Layout section of Word.
- Only use the top half of each page – so your head doesn't dip down when you are reading. Your eyes will move down, but your head will not.
- Double-space – so you don't have any trouble finding your place.
- Use a larger font – 14 or 16 point will do.
- Don't type in all caps – all caps are hard to read.
- Use subheadings to separate one idea from the next.
- Use an ellipsis (…) or a slash (/) between sentences that need a pause for effect.
- Bold or underline a word or phrase that needs extra emphasis.
- Number your pages in a contrasting color like red, handwriting them with a marker so you clearly can see the page number.
- When there is no lectern to lay your script on, staple the pages together on the top left-hand corner and hold the document up to the top of the document, so it is in line with your nose. This will again help you be able to read the words and look out at your audience without moving your head up.
- When you do have a lectern set the pages down on the right side of the lectern and move the first page over to the left. Now you have page 1 and page 2 in front of you. As you finish page 2, move that page over to the left, so you now have page 2 and page 3 in front of you, and so forth.

You are halfway there when the first draft of the written script is completed. I say the first draft because as you begin to rehearse the text, you will be making changes to words used, what to emphasize, where to pause, and adding and taking away content to the speech. So what do you do next?

Reading the written script:

- Take the time to read over the speech 50 times before its delivery. Not 25 times or 40 times, but 50 times. This will naturally have you recalling specific passages from memory without intentionally having to do so. You are not trying to memorize the script; you are merely getting familiar with the content, so you will be able to look up at the audience for a more extended period of time while naturally recalling what words are coming next without looking back to the pages.

- Look up as much as possible – you don't want to lose that connection with your audience.
- Read with pride – don't apologize for reading it.
- Sound as if you mean it – even if you don't. We all have to give speeches that we don't want to give or don't always agree with. It's too late to back out now, so fake it if you must.
- Pause as much as you can. It gives you time to look at your script. A pause may feel like a lifetime to you the speaker, but the listeners don't have that same experience. A pause is your best way of sounding authoritative.
- Pause before and after a key phrase or message. It increases the impact.

Finally, in this regard, President Ronald Reagan, the 40th president of the United States, who has been referred to as "The Great Communicator," used the "see, stop, and say" method when forced to read a speech without a teleprompter (Figure 4.12).[21]

- See – See each phrase and "record" a picture of it with your eyes. Instead of reading the whole section, let your eye "record" only the phrase or part of the phrase that you can commit to memory.
- Stop – Look up from the page and pause.
- Say – Say the phrase out loud from visual memory. Pause again before looking down to memorize the next phrase.

Figure 4.12 President Ronald Reagan reading a television speech to the nation. (From Shutterstock.)

PRESENTING WITH AN INTERPRETER

The challenge of working with an interpreter during any oral speaking engagement requires a lot of planning and know-how. I have had several occasions to experience the use of interpreters, and it quickly became evident that I had to work closely with the interpreter to be successful. Generally, there are two types of interpreters that you will run into. The first is the professional interpreter, who does this for a living, and the second is the subject matter expert interpreter, who is familiar with the subject and speaks the language of the audience. If you have the option, always go with the professional interpreter over a subject matter expert. The professional interpreter has the communication skills necessary to help you accomplish your objectives. They may not have the grasp of the subject being presented, but they do have the knowledge, skills, and abilities to effectively communicate what you are presenting promptly and accurately. The subject matter expert doesn't always have those skills. They tend not to be interpreters at all, but only someone in your field who can speak the language and happened to be available at the time of the event.

I experienced being a plenary speaker at the New Developments in Criminal Justice Conference in China in 2004. The audience of approximately 150 attendees were all Chinese and to my knowledge none understood English. All the attendees were wearing headsets, and the interpreters were listening to me speak in English that was immediately translated into the official language of China, which is Mandarin. I never met the interpreters. They were sitting in a booth in the back of the hall. I don't know what they looked like. I was never told if they were professional interpreters or criminal justice professionals. The only instruction I was given was to talk slowly. How slowly or whether I was speaking slowly enough for the interpreters, I had no idea. All I know was that I had 150 plus attendees looking at me for an hour, and I had no idea if they understood a word I said.

My second experience with an interpreter was with a hearing-impaired student I had in my academic class at the university. At every class, twice a week, the university provided two professional sign language interpreters for her while I was presenting a 3-hour lecture each day. The interpreters took turns every 15 minutes. The only time I had to prepare the interpreters for something special was when I was having an unannounced demonstration of a mock robbery committed in the classroom. The lights in the lecture hall would go out for a few seconds, there would be screaming in the room, the lights would come back on, and a mock robbery would be committed in the front of the classroom. The robber would steal a student's computer and run out of the room. The whole event took approximately 15 to 20 seconds. One problem was that the hearing-impaired student would see the lights go out but not hear the screaming, so when the lights went back on, she would not have any reference point to consider. The interpreter suggested that he would draw her attention to the front of the room when the lights went back on. This planning proved acceptable for all concerned and the hearing-impaired student was actively engaged in the event as a result. Other than that one situation, having the sign language interpreters in the room did not require any special attention on my part. If she had a question or wanted to comment, the interpreters handled both very smoothly.

The most recent experience I had with an interpreter was when I was lecturing to a class of Chinese police officers in my crime laboratory classroom. The interpreter was Chinese, from China, and was one of our criminal justice graduate students. He was not a professional interpreter, and forensic sciences were not his area of expertise. He asked if he could have access to my PowerPoint slides so he could translate them and include the translations below each of the English words on the slides. This provided to be an excellent idea. I did have to adjust the slides to get the extra Chinese text on them, but it worked out favorably. As you can see in Figure 4.13, I have the interpreter standing beside me at the podium. I continued to be the principal speaker, while the interpreter translates in the background.

Those are three situations you may come across when presenting to an audience having to use an interpreter. Now let's provide you with some general guidelines that will assist you when the time comes for you to be using an interpreter. The following guidance will help you in your preparation and delivery:

- Speak slowly in short sound bites and enunciate. Discuss how slow that needs to be with the interpreter. Each burst of content you say should be a complete thought.
- Taking questions. Discuss with the interpreter when to take questions from the audience. It may be best to handle specific questions when they have them, to clear up any translation issue that may be happening without you knowing. Otherwise, general questions are best taken at the end of the session.

Figure 4.13   Professor Mauriello lecturing to police officers from China with an interpreter by his side. (Photo courtesy of the Office of International and Executive Programs (OIEP) at the University of Maryland. Photo taken by Michael Dravis.)

- Prepare less material for the time allotted. It takes longer to convey your information with an interpreter, so work with the interpreter to decide on the amount of content you can successfully present within the time frame allotted.
- Discuss with the interpreter your use of terminology, idioms, and metaphors. Make sure the interpreter understands all the technical terms you will be using. Try to reduce or even eliminate your use of idioms and metaphors, because these word combinations have different symbolic meaning than the literal meaning of each word or phrase. That causes more confusion than it's worth.
- Use humor carefully. The use of humor in public speaking is an excellent technique for gaining rapport with any audience. You do have to be careful though with international audiences. You have to make sure that the humor is appropriate and culturally acceptable.

There is one final point that needs to be mentioned. It is when you are told that your audience can understand and speak your language, and therefore the tasker will not be providing you with an interpreter. This can be dangerous. Trust me; it has happened to me on two occasions. It appeared that the audiences could understand me speaking English pretty well, or at least much better than I could understand them when they were trying to speak in English when asking questions. I could not understand them, and it became frustrating for both me and the audiences. Ask for someone who can translate for you if needed. You will be glad you did.

The criminal justice and forensic sciences communities have several international organizations including the American Academy of Forensic Sciences (AAFS), International Association of Identification (IAI), and International Association of Chiefs of Police, to name a few. These organizations have members from worldwide countries that speak many different languages. These organizations give their members opportunities to speak to these very diverse audiences, so consider the preceding information before presenting.

CHAPTER REVIEW REFLECTION TOOLS

1. The least effective method for learning is listening to spoken words.
2. The most effective methods for learning involve direct, hands-on interactive activities with the audience.
3. Visual slides should augment spoken words.
4. The speaker should be the center of attention.
5. The speaker should be the focus of the audience's attention, not the PowerPoint slides.
6. Consider the 6/30 rule – 6 slides per 30 minutes of oral presentation.
7. Use a font that is easy on the eyes and easy to read.
8. The average font size should be 24 point, larger for titles.
9. Don't use dark-colored fonts with dark-colored backgrounds.
10. 6×6 Presentation Rule for slides – six words per line and no more than six bullet points per slide.
11. Don't read your slides to the audience unless you are trying to emphasize something on a slide.
12. Limit the length of video clips from 30 seconds to 5–7 minutes.
13. To prepare to read a speech, read it over 50 times before presenting it.
14. When using a language interpreter, meet with them beforehand.

NOTES

1. Ray Semko is a retired federal agent, security educator, and a professional public speaker who is internationally known for his popular and motivating D*I*C*E security awareness and counterintelligence briefings, which he has been presenting to American audiences worldwide for over 30 years. See https://raysemko.com/.

2. Edgar Dale, *Audio-Visual Methods in Teaching*, 3rd ed., Holt, Rinehart & Winston, New York, 1969, p. 108.
3. Dr. Michael Martin Hammer was an American engineer, management author, and a former professor of computer science at the Massachusetts Institute of Technology, known as one of the founders of the management theory of business process reengineering.
4. A viewgraph is a graphic or textual image on a transparency for use with an overhead projector to be viewed on a screen.
5. Microsoft PowerPoint is a slideshow presentation program first developed by Forethought, Inc., for the Macintosh computer in 1987 and purchased by Microsoft in 1990.
6. The "pre-briefing package" used to be a series of documents provided to the audience of a briefing prior to its presentation. It gave the audience some background information on the subject area and saved valuable briefing time. When PowerPoint got popular, the pre-briefing package became the briefing slides only. That in turn required that briefer to include more information on the slides than necessary.
7. Nuts & Bolts, "9 Safe PowerPoint Fonts that Work in All Versions of PowerPoint," Nuts & Bolts for PowerPoint, https://nutsandboltsspeedtraining.com/powerpoint-tutorials/safe-fonts-powerpoint/.
8. I don't agree with her by the way.
9. Noah Zandan, "Color Psychology – What Colors Make Great Presentations?" Quantified Communications, www.quantifiedcommunications.com/blog/color-psychology-what-colors-make-great-presentations/.
10. Cliff Atkinson, *Beyond Bullet Points: Using Microsoft PowerPoint to Create Presentations That Inform, Motive, and Inspire*, Microsoft Press, 2005.
11. Many new facilities with integrated audio/visual equipment installed in them will have a large flat screen installed on the wall in the back of the room so the speaker can look straight out into the audience and at the same time view their slides.
12. PowerPoint has about 16 different types of transitions to go from one slide to the next. Some are very dramatic and not appropriate for a business-type presentation.
13. For additional information on how the brain absorbs information and the concept of mind mapping in all forms of live, see the following book: Tony Buzan, *Mind Map Mastery: The Complete Guide to Learning and Using the Most Powerful Thinking Tool in the Universe*, Watkins, 2018.
14. A hyperlink is an icon, graphic, or text in a slide that will link to another slide, program file, internet, video clip, or other media. You can link to different places in a presentation, such as the first slide, last slide, next slide, or slide titles. All you have to do is highlight the object or word you want to hyperlink from and right-click. A window pops up and you will see "hyperlink" listed. Click on it and select where you want to link to. You always want to return to the Mind Map from that location.

15. Copyright on YouTube is an important topic for the YouTube community. See the following uniform resource locator (URL) to find out how to manage your rights and learn more about respecting the rights of others: www.youtube.com/about/copyright/#support-and-troubleshooting.
16. An icebreaker can be a story, a joke (although not recommended here), or some other form of information that is presented to build rapport with the audience.
17. See www.bitlaw.com/copyright/index.html for a review of the federal copyright laws.
18. See note 3.
19. A learning management system (LMS) is a software application or web-based technology used to plan, implement, and assess a specific learning process. Typically, a learning management system provides an instructor with a way to create and deliver content, monitor student participation, and assess student performance. It is basically a one-stop shopping location for the students to obtain all the content they need to successfully pass a course.
20. A plenary session is a session delivered at a conference where all attendees of the conference are invited to attend.
21. Claire Doole, "How to Sound Natural When Reading a Speech," February 27, 2017, www.doolecommunications.com/sound-natural-reading-speech/.

5

Evolution of Presentation Audio/ Visual (A/V) Technology

INTRODUCTION

Chapter 5 provides the reader with a historical perspective of the evolution of audio/visual (A/V) presentation technologies used in the past, current ones used in the present, and those that should not be used anymore in the future. Technology is moving the traditional brick-and-mortar presentations out into the virtual world. As a result, this chapter discusses how today's audio/visual devices can make that happen seamlessly for public speakers and educators. Finally, this chapter provides a valuable list of A/V connection devices needed by the professional speaker to ensure their computer system is compatible with all the technologies installed at the site where they may be speaking. Even virtual presentations need hard-wired technologies to help speakers deliver their message.

CHALKBOARDS AND FLIP CHARTS TO OVERHEAD PROJECTORS

I began my public speaking and teaching career when there was no audio/ visual technology being used regularly on the podium, and the only visuals a speaker could use were written by hand on chalkboards, flip charts,[1] and transparencies[2] using an overhead projector (Figures 5.1 to 5.3).

Figure 5.1 Flipcharts. (From Shutterstock.)

Figure 5.2 Chalkboards. (From Shutterstock.)

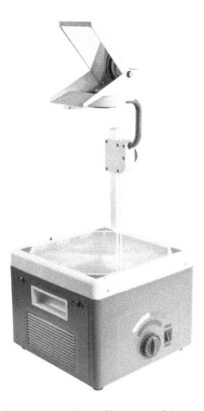

Figure 5.3 Overhead projectors. (From Shutterstock.)

For the most part, these items worked as long as the speaker had excellent writing skills, and the room wasn't too large for the audience to see what was being written. The overhead projector eliminated the problem of the information being too small because the image on the screen could be enlarged as needed. The problem was that when the speaker laid the transparency on the overhead projector, it was never straight and was a distraction for the viewer. The other issue for all three methods was that the speaker had to turn their back to the audience when using the chalkboard or flip chart or to wade through the speaker's pile of transparencies to pick the one they wanted to project next. The flip chart and whiteboards (which replaced the chalkboard and uses markers instead of chalk) still have their place in rooms with small groups of participants. The overhead projector is all but done or should be gone. If there is anyone still out there using overhead transparencies to communicate their presentation, they are telling their audience that they have not updated their presentation for years and that they just don't care.

16MM FILM TO THE VIDEO CASSETTE RECORDER (VCR)

In the 1970s and early '80s, the only audio/visual devices that could project movies or training films was the 16mm film projector. I remember lugging around a 16mm projector to my classroom to show several training films that I had integrated into my lectures. I had to drive 40 miles to obtain the films that were the possession of the Maryland Police Training Commission. The following day I had to drive them back. Because films were hard to get and inconvenient to have available when you needed them, and because venues didn't always have 16mm projectors available, speakers tended not to consider using them in their presentations (Figure 5.4).

Figure 5.4 16mm film projector. (From Shutterstock.)

Also during the early 1970s there began a slow shift away from 16mm film with Sony's introduction of the 3/4 inch U-matic Video Cassette Recorder (VCR) for commercial use. 16mm films were being transferred onto 3/4 video cassettes and projected with video projectors onto a screen. The problem at the time was that video projectors were far from perfected and didn't have the clarity that the 16mm projector had. The other problem was that speakers and trainers alike tended to overuse this new technology and were filling a lot of valuable speaker time with too much video. I will say this over and over again in this book, "Too much of anything is too much." Even with today's technology and high-tech video systems, short video clips 30 seconds to 5 minutes long are best to augment a presentation (Figure 5.5).

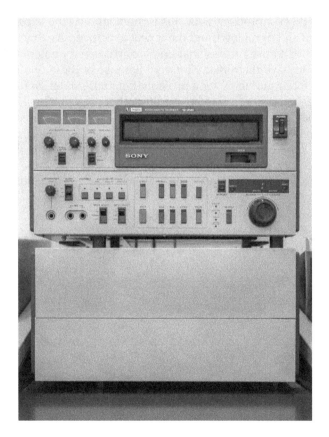

Figure 5.5 Sony U-matic VCR. (From Shutterstock.)

35MM SLIDE PROJECTORS TO POWERPOINT SLIDES AND VIDEO PROJECTORS

During this same period, the 35mm slide projector became the mainstay for public speakers and teachers. The projector contained a series of 35mm small slides, positive pieces of film, typically about 1.375 inches by .875 inches, held by rectangles of cardboard or plastic so that they end up as 2-inch squares. They provided the speaker with clear, sharp images projected on a screen or a smooth white wall at any size needed for audiences to easily view. All you had to do is change the lens to project the image for small or large rooms. The slides were placed in a circular container called a carousel. You had to turn the slide upside down and counterclockwise to put it in a numbered slot in the carousel. The slides had to be projected in a linear fashion, one at a time. The biggest problem with this technology was the expense to have them created and developed, and the time it took to receive them for presentation. You had to use professional graphic artists and photographers, who took weeks to have them ready for you. Because of these two issues, after slides were made and used for a presentation, those slides would be stored in special racked containers to be used for other presentations. Many times a speaker would use a slide that wasn't exactly what they wanted or needed, but in the interest of saving money and time, it was used (Figure 5.6).

As we approached the 21st century, the one thing that significantly affected the way we presented oral communications was the integration of computer systems hardware and PowerPoint presentation software,

Figure 5.6 35mm slide projector. (From Shutterstock.)

projected with more vivid video projector technology. Speakers can now create, produce, and present audio/visual presentations on their own rather than bare the expense and time to have other professionals do that for them. For those speakers who may not be as computer savvy as they would like, there is help all around you. The workplace usually has folks that provide that service or can assist you, and teachers can get that same help from their students, and don't forget your children and grandchildren. They have grown up with all these technologies. Using computers and software programs are second nature to them. Additional capabilities that these technologies gave the speaker integrated into a PowerPoint program are (Figure 5.7)

- Embedded audio sounds – For sound effects or audio from video
- Embedded video clips – As part of the PowerPoint program
- Live internet connection to content and video programs (for example, YouTube) – Hyperlink from the PowerPoint program directly to an internet source (You obviously have to have internet access)
- Hyperlink capability to other presentations – Other PowerPoint programs, Word or PDF[3] documents, etc.
- Capability to store files on mobile devices (CDs, DVDs, thumb drives, networks)

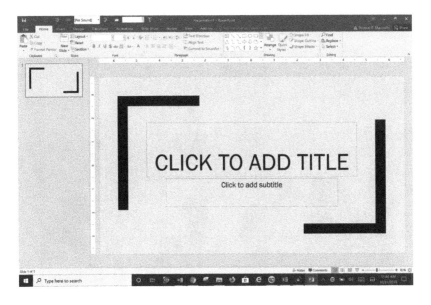

Figure 5.7 PowerPoint presentation software. (Created by T. P. Mauriello.)

LIVE PRESENTATIONS TO VIDEO TELECONFERENCING

It doesn't appear that technology is going to eliminate the use of live platform-type presentations in the near future. That's a good thing because technology has already reduced today's generation's ability to communicate with one another when they are standing or sitting next to each other. I don't know what is ahead, so I never say never. What I do know is that a lot of live meetings and presentations can be replaced effectively and efficiently with video teleconferencing technology to get the same results. For example, right now, as I am writing this section of this book, I am preparing to give a lecture to my students via Skype.[4] I am in sunny Florida overlooking the Gulf of Mexico, while my students will be looking at me on two monitors in my crime lab at the University of Maryland. I will be able to see all the students, and they will be able to see me. We can talk to each other, and I will also be able to share my computer screen if I need them to view any PowerPoint slides or other content during my lecture. This is not a common occurrence for my class, but I had business in Florida, and I didn't want to cancel the class. There are many video teleconference programs besides Skype that are available. GoToMeeting®, Zoom Video Communications, GlobalMeet® Video Conferencing, Cisco Webex Meetings, and BlueJeans Meetings, to name a few (Figure 5.8).

Figure 5.8   Video teleconferencing. (From Shutterstock.)

LECTURE HALLS AND CLASSROOMS TO
THE VIDEO RECORDING STUDIO

Lecture halls and classrooms as we have known them are being replaced at a relatively slow pace with rooms that are quite different in space, size, type, and placement of furniture, and instructor and student technology. The University of Maryland at College Park recently opened their doors to the brand-new Edward St. John Learning & Teaching Center that supports team-based and collaborative modes of teaching and learning with spaces that satisfy those new requirements. The goal in developing these spaces is to promote student-centered teaching practices by creating technology-enhanced environments that enable every person in the classroom to teach, engage, respond, and participate. The types of rooms that are replacing the traditional lecture hall and classroom are referred to as "tiered collaborative rooms" that have specialized fixed-seating arranged on tiers that are two rows deep (see Figure 5.9). These new rooms allow students in each pair of rows to collaborate around a central table for team-based exercises. "6Round" (see Figure 5.10) spaces are designed without a primary teaching wall, with round tables where students sit in groups of six throughout the area. The instructor's station is in the middle of the room and marker boards are situated on the perimeter walls adjacent to each of the round tables. One projection screen on each of the four walls allows viewing of up to two images simultaneously from any seat in the room. The "media share" (see Figure 5.11) rooms have peninsula-style student tables that flank the outer walls of the room. Each station is equipped with a computer where students may work together on projects in groups of six and share content via the screens with the entire class through a dynamic software package. "Huddle rooms" (see Figure 5.12) are similar to traditional conference rooms where students can have meetings, work on class projects, or connect with collaborators around the world.

Figure 5.9 Tiered collaborative room. (Photo by John T. Consoli/University of Maryland [ESJLTC_Interiors_01162018 0495].)

Figure 5.10 6round space. (Photo by John T. Consoli/University of Maryland [ESJLTC_Interiors_01162018 0495].)

Figure 5.11 Media share room. (Photo by John T. Consoli/University of Maryland [ESJLTC_Interiors_01162018 0495].)

Figure 5.12 Huddle room. (Photo by John T. Consoli/University of Maryland [ESJLTC_Interiors_01162018 0495].)

For many of us, the audiences we speak to today have been learning quite differently than we have. We can fight them or join them, depending on our interest in success. What I have always loved about public speaking and teaching is being able to speak to large groups of people either in a lecture hall or auditorium – the bigger, the better. I was comfortable with my ability to engage an audience, have them asking questions, and making comments during the event. That all changed in 2012. Thankfully at the same time, I was retiring from my full-time government position and had more time to deal with it.

I began to notice that I was getting less and less engagement from my student audiences. They stopped asking questions and making comments like they always had done. They began sending me emails and then text messages asking me questions about my lecture that they left just hours before. They were usually valid questions that needed my clarification, but when I did that, the students who sent me the electronic questions were the only ones benefiting from my answers. If the student who was asking the question didn't understand, who else in the class didn't understand. I tried to encourage them to ask questions in class, to no avail. My frustration got worse when one evening in class, several students were sound asleep in the middle of the room. They were making no effort to hide their total disregard for what I was doing in front of them. I stopped in midsentence and asked those students who were sleeping to wake up, move to the back of the lecture hall if they had to, or just leave totally. I am confident that my irritation was apparent. At the class break, one of those students sleeping came up to me and respectfully asked me why I was upset with him sleeping. He said he wasn't really sleeping; he just had his eyes closed. I looked at him in amazement and laughed, but then realized he was serious. He continued by telling me that he was getting the information, and even wanted to show me his notes. He was not trying to be disrespectful and was trying to say to me that he was getting the material. He just wanted to get it on his terms.

That evening I reflected on what I was experiencing. It appeared that I was the only one talking in the lecture hall and that I needed to do something different to regain the same attention and engagement I had enjoyed from my students in the past years. That's when I left what I loved, lecturing in the large lecture hall, and moved my classroom lectures to a virtual space. I recorded all my lectures and placed them on the university's learning management system website. See Chapter 10 and learn about how I transformed my class into a flipped classroom and blended learning formatted course.

I spent 6 months videotaping all my lectures into 81 short video clips. The university suggested videotaping me lecturing first in their studio and then integrating my slides with the video afterward. I didn't agree. It was bad enough that I would be lecturing to a camera, not an audience; I believed it would be more challenging to lecture without the aid of the slides at my side. The result was I created my own studio in my home office, learned to use a video-editing software program and video editor that would allow me to record myself lecturing and my slides at the same time, and then after I could produce a final recording of both images as I saw fit. I was able to create a recording that simulated everything that I was doing live on the podium. The recording shows both me and my slides, just me, just my slides, and any video clips that I was using. If I used a video that required discussion in the middle of the video, the recording views the video paused and me appearing on the screen engaged in a discussion. What this did for my class was allowed the students to receive the content of a module at home at their leisure, and then we all come into the crime laboratory and spent 100% of the lab time engaging in practical hands-on exercises that demonstrated their knowledge of what they had learned.

Yes, I had to get comfortable lecturing to a camera all alone in my small office studio, but after a while, I was able to visualize the students watching me, listening to my every word. And if they didn't understand what I said, they could stop the video and rerun it and listen again. That is a good thing. The bad thing is you better have your content right because your audience will call you on anything contrary to what you said previously. This is where we are now, so you either fight it or embrace it. I suggest you embrace it and transmit the knowledge you all have in a manner acceptable to the listeners. Your audiences will be glad you did.

PREPARING AUDIO/VISUAL (A/V) EQUIPMENT FOR PRESENTATIONS

A/V technology is impressive when it works. Before today's technology was available, the only thing you had to worry about was whether the bulb in the projector was working. There was one switch to flip, the on/off switch to the slide, overhead, or 16mm projector. If you flipped it and nothing happened, you knew it was the bulb, and you replaced it. Today it is more complicated. We use software to drive content, contained in a computer, that is connected to a projector and audio system. All these items have to work in unison. There are two operating systems that are available today, PC and Mac. A PC[5] generally refers to a computer that runs on a Windows operating system.

The Mac runs on an Apple, Inc. operating system. Both operating systems have operational advantages over the other reference the quality of what is seen on the screen, but that doesn't satisfy compatibility issues when attempting to connect all the equipment in the presentation room. I can confidently tell you that most presentation rooms, such as a classroom, meeting room, conference room, ballroom, hotel or restaurant function hall, etc., use PC equipment with a Windows operating system. That doesn't mean you can't connect a Mac computer to the system, but it does mean there are sometimes compatibility issues because of it. When I have a student or speaker complain of compatibility issues with their computers, 90% of the time, it is because they have a Mac computer.

So what do you need to do to ensure that your technology works when you are ready to give your speech, lecture, or training presentation? Never trust your equipment to work the way you believe it should. It is up to you and you only to make sure you have done everything in your power for it to work the way you expect. There are three steps that must be completed far in advance before your time to present, but not too far in advance where some new problem could arise after your successful test.

- Step 1: Connect it. If you have an option, use a PC with a Windows operating system. You will have a better chance of compatibility. Next, don't rely on the room where you are speaking to have the correct connections between your equipment and their equipment. Always bring your own patch cords, extenders, multioutlet electrical power extender, and presentation remote control. Today's new slimline laptop computers have fewer ports to plug in A/V equipment. They may only have one USB port and maybe a mini HDMI port. The only way you plug a project into your laptop would be with an A/V adapter. See Figures 5.13 to 5.18.
- Step 2: Test it. Test all the equipment you intend to use during your presentation. Do not make the mistake of just testing your equipment at home or work. If you are not testing all the equipment you will be using during your presentation, then you are not correctly satisfying this task. Trust me. I have made this mistake before.
- Step 3: Use it. I mean, just don't turn the equipment on and off to ensure power is working. I say turn everything on, and I mean everything. Then go through your slides to make sure the resolution on the screen is correct; if you embedded audio in one or more of the slides, go to each of those slides to make sure the audio can be heard; if you intend to use the internet, make sure you can connect to the room's network properly. Don't let someone tell you

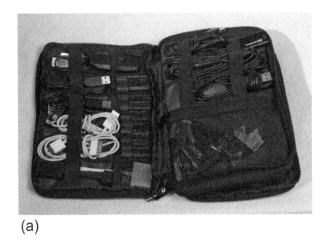

(a)

Figure 5.13a Double-fold A/V accessory container (left side). (Photo by Luiz Santos.)

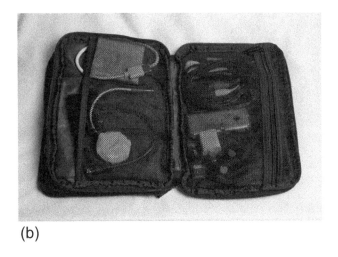

(b)

Figure 5.13b Double-fold A/V accessory container (right side). (Photo by Luiz Santos.)

Figure 5.14 Multi-plug electric power cube and extender. (Photo by Luiz Santos.)

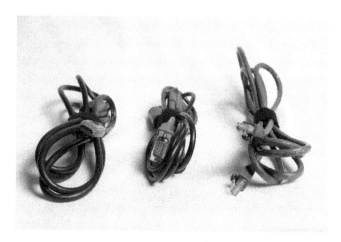

Figure 5.15 Mini plug audio–VGA video–ethernet–HDMI cables. (Photo by Luiz Santos.)

that it will work unless you personally see it work. Remember, you will be the only one standing at the podium to blame if something goes wrong.

Now you are ready to present, speak, talk, teach, lecture, argue, and testify, with the confidence that your technology will be working with you.

Figure 5.16   Mini HDMI to VGA and HDMI cable. (Photo by Luiz Santos.)

Figure 5.17   USB to ethernet and three USB cable adapters. (Photo by Luiz Santos.)

The figures are photographs of A/V equipment a professional speaker should have with them at all times. The equipment are all mine, and they are used all the time. I can't tell you how many times I have been to a venue where they did not have the proper cables or adapters to connect my laptop to their system.

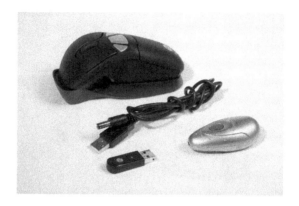

Figure 5.18   Presentation remote control – laser pointer. (Photo by Luiz Santos.)

CHAPTER REVIEW REFLECTION TOOLS

1. A/V equipment should assist the speaker in presenting a speech, not be in place of it.
2. The traditional lecture is being replaced with blended learning methods.
3. Make sure that your A/V hardware and software is compatible with your equipment and the equipment in the room where you are presenting.
4. Test and retest your A/V equipment before your presentation.

NOTES

1. A flip chart is a large pad of paper bound so that each page can be turned over at the top to reveal the next, used on a stand at presentations.
2. A transparency, also referred to as a viewgraph, is a thin sheet of transparent flexible material, typically cellulose acetate, onto which images can be drawn, or text or other documents could be photocopied onto the transparency. These are then placed on an overhead projector to be shown on a projection screen for display to an audience.
3. PDF stands for "portable document format." It allows you to share documents between computers and across operating system platforms when you need to save files that cannot be modified.
4. Skype is a Microsoft telecommunications application that specializes in providing video chat and voice calls between computers, tablets, and mobile devices.
5. PC stands for "personal computer." Generically any computer that is a stand alone could be considered a PC, but technically it stands for a computer with a Windows operating system.

6

Surveying the Venue Where You Will Be Speaking

INTRODUCTION

This chapter focuses on the physical location used for the presentation and the audio/visual (A/V) equipment installed. Careful and deliberate preparation is vital in this regard. It is recommended you visit the site before presentation day; survey the type of A/V equipment installed and the type of connections used; the location of electrical power outlets; how to use your laptop or the desktop in the facility; evaluate the use of audio speakers and microphone equipment to be "heard" and "understood" by all in attendance; and, finally, determine the floor plan where the placement of the podium, projector screen, and attendee's desks, tables, and chairs are best located. In the event your presentation is transmitted via a teleconference system, this chapter details what the speaker must know to successfully project visuals and their image out to the live audience and attendees at virtual locations. All these logistical details can make or break your presentation.

PHYSICAL SPACE

At the same time that you are planning your presentation, creating the content, and determining what format you will be using, you need to know what the physical space will look like where you will be presenting.

To do this, you must have an idea of how many attendees will be present and how you want them to be seated. For example, the following are several seating styles that speakers come across when asked to speak to an audience (also see Figure 6.1):

Seating Styles

- Theater
- Classroom
- U-shape
- Boardroom
- Banquet
- Cabaret

Additional styles based on availability

- Cocktail – Attendees standing up where cocktails and hors d'oeuvres are served.
- Lounge – A nightclub lounge is also used for presentations. (For example, cruise ships use their nightclub lounges during the day for presentations and training programs.)

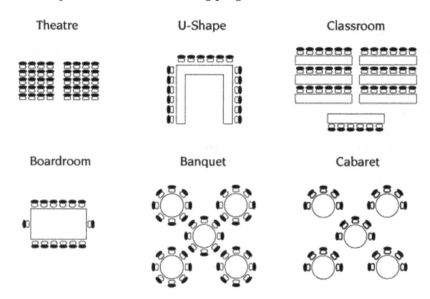

Figure 6.1 Seating styles.

LOCATION OF PODIUM, LECTERN, A/V CONNECTIONS, AND PROJECTION SCREEN

The speaker stands on a *podium* and stands behind a *lectern*, so let us use these terms correctly. The podium may be a small platform or stage in front of the audience or the ground-level floor in front of the audience. The lectern is a stand-alone piece of furniture for the speaker to stand behind and is a place for their laptop computer, notes, and a microphone. The lectern can also be a slanted tabletop model that sits on a table. It contains electrical power and A/V and microphone connections. The projection screen should be located on or near the podium. The speaker should pay particular attention to where these four items (i.e., podium, lectern, A/V connections, and projection screen) are located. Why? Because sometimes poor planning finds that these four items are in different locations, making it difficult for the speaker to present in a comfortable position for the speaker and the audience.

The screen should be as close to the speaker as possible, as shown in Figure 6.2. In large ballrooms and auditoriums with hundreds of seats, the large oversized screens tend to be nowhere near the speaker. The result is the audience looking like they are on the sideline of a tennis match with their heads moving back and forth from the speaker to the screen back to the speaker. The companies that supply and install the screens make no attempt to place the screens in a location that is beneficial to the audience participants. You find multiple screens in the corners of the room, a far distance from the podium and lectern. In the event you the speaker has

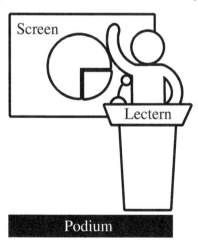

Figure 6.2 Podium, lectern, screen. (From Shutterstock.)

any influence not to let this happen, take that advantage. Next, project one of your PowerPoint slides on the screen and physically walk to the far corners of the room to ensure you can read the text. You may recall in Chapter 4 that I recommend using 24 point font size with no less than 18 point. The determination on how large the projection screen should be in any given room can be calculated by visiting Projector Screen.com and use the projection screen calculator on that site. It will help you determine the following:[1]

- The viewable area of a screen based on any one dimension.
- Throw distance and optimal screen size based on your projector.
- Optimal seating distance for your audience based on the projector screen size you are considering.

Although many believe that all you have to do is give a speaker a wireless remote and not worry about where the A/V connections are for your laptop; this proves time and again to be a wrong. If you are using hyperlinks in your PowerPoint presentation or going from a PowerPoint slide to a video show or onto the internet, having laptop control is a must. You also want to have your laptop in front of you so you can see what is projected on the screen without turning around and having your back to the audience.

PODIUM AND ROOM LIGHTING

The lighting in the room has so much to do with how your presentation is received, yet it generally is not considered by the contractor who designed the room and determined where and what type of lighting would be installed. The rule of thumb is you want as much light as possible on the entire audience for you to see the whites of the eyes of the audience attendees in the back of the room. Placing the audience in a darkened room only puts them into an altered state of consciousness or sleep. If you are lucky, the light fixtures in the room are in tiers and on dimmers with each row of lighting on separate switches. That way, you can reduce the lighting directly in front of the projection screen and turn the lights up higher in the rest of the room. You don't want the lighting to wash out the slides on the screen. That is becoming less of a problem with the new laser projectors that use laser technology rather than projection bulbs.

Take the time to test the lights and see what is best for the room. A problem that I have encountered is with the newer built or redesigned rooms that have preset light dimmers. They don't allow you to set the dimmer at a level you want. You will see choices like full, 75%, 50%, and off. This is another example of contractors and IT folks who build these facilities, never talking to the end-user, the speaker.

Once many years ago, I traveled to one of my agency's field sites in the continental United States. The field site didn't have a large staff contingency, so anytime anyone from headquarters was traveling there for business, if the traveler was a trainer who could offer one of their courses for the employees there, they were asked to do so. I was asked to present one of my four-hour seminars. When I got there, I found out that the training officer forgot to make the announcement that I was coming and was offering the training. In order not to be embarrassed, the commander ordered a group of 20 military service personnel to come off their leave and required them to attend the course. I was not aware of this at the time. While I was preparing the room for the training, I found out that there was only one light switch in the room and it controlled all the lights. In other words, the lights were either on or off. The room had no windows or any other source for lighting. I would be putting 20 human beings, who were being forced to attend a training session on their day off, in the dark for four hours. Not a chance. The light fixtures were multiple fluorescent tubes. So I found a ladder and unscrewed every other tube in every light fixture in the room. The alternative would have been deadly.

THE USE OF A MICROPHONE WHEN SPEAKING

To repeat, as we have been saying throughout this book, the objective of any good speaker is to be "heard, understood, and remembered." Let's deal with one of the five human senses of being "heard." The sensing organs associated with each sense send information to the brain to help us understand and perceive the world around us. Hearing is essential to oral communication because it is the main feeder of information to the brain as the speaker is talking. It doesn't matter how loud or strong your voice may be; the size of the room and the size of the audience can affect the acoustics in the room, which ultimately affects the audience's ability to hear the speaker. Without getting into the technical aspects of a microphone, all a speaker needs to know is when and how to use one and what type. Ask someone familiar with the venue whether microphones are generally used. You don't want to have to scream to be heard, so if you are not sure whether it is necessary, use it. When you are testing out the size of the fonts on your slides and going to the back of the room, also check to ensure you can be heard either with or without a microphone. It is not the time to do this when the audience is there in the room. Don't use the audience to do this testing. Do it before they come into the room.

The best type of microphone for a speaker who wants to be engaging their audience is a lavalier microphone. A lavalier microphone or lavalier (also known as a lav, lapel mic, clip mic, body mic, collar mic, or personal mic) is a small microphone used for public speaking applications to allow for hands-free operation. It allows for total movability by the speaker. The lavalier is wireless, but there is a small unit that must be attached somewhere on the speaker's body with a wire that extends from the clip-on unit to the microphone that is clipped to the center of the speaker's chest area close to the mouth (Figure 6.3 and Figure 6.4). This is an easy process for a male speaker because no matter what he may be wearing, he will have a belt or pocket to hold the unit to his body. A woman, on the other hand, has to do a little planning to be able to attach both the unit and the mic itself on what she is wearing. There is a solution. I see more and more headset wireless microphones that are placed around your head and over your ears. The microphone is then placed to the side of your mouth. See Figure 6.5.

Most microphones are now wireless, although you still see some wired microphones mounted on a lectern. Microphones attached to the

Figure 6.3 Lavalier microphone. (From Shutterstock.)

Figure 6.4   Lavalier microphone. (From Shutterstock.)

Figure 6.5   Headset mic. (From Shutterstock.)

lectern require the speaker to be tied to the lectern. It limits their ability to move away from the podium. Once you decide to use a microphone, there should be no going back. Problems exist when the microphone is attached to the lectern on the opposite side of the projection screen, so when you turn to view the screen, you are turning away from the mic. The change in sound level becomes an irritant for the audience who hears your voice going in and out of the audio speakers. Sometimes it is best not to use a mic at all when the only mic available is stationary on the lectern. If you chose not to use a hot mic (one that is on), then shut it off.

Handheld wireless microphones are the worst for speakers. You must hold it in your hand and close to your mouth. See Figure 6.6. On one hand, the speaker is holding the wireless mic and on the other hand, he is holding a remote control device. When we talk about hand gestures and nonverbal communications in Chapter 7, you will realize how that limits you from communicating effectively.

DOWNLOADING PRESENTATION CONTENT INTO ROOM COMPUTER SYSTEMS

First, let me tell you I never do it. Experience has shown me that if you want potential technical problems to be increased, then download your PowerPoint program into a computer system in the room where you are speaking and hope for the best. If your PowerPoint program has nothing but simple slides without embedded audio and video clips, then everything will probably be ok. But even then, if you created your slides with a different version of PowerPoint that is not supported in the computer system in the room you are speaking at, your hyperlinks or slide transitions will not always work as you planned. You have control over your laptop computer. You do not have any control over the computer that is not yours. Always consider using your own laptop.

Figure 6.6 Hand-held mic. (From Shutterstock.)

TELEPRESENCE VIDEOCONFERENCING PRESENTATIONS

Telepresence videoconferencing is a two-way, high-definition communi-cation and collaboration tool. It allows the presenter the ability to com-municate to both a live and distant audience in such a way as if they were all in the same room. Through the use of video cameras, monitors/projec-tors, and microphones at both ends, and using one of the many telecom-munications applications[2] available via the internet, presenters can now be anywhere at any time and reach the desired audience. As the speaker, you do not need to know what is behind the scenes that accomplish this collaboration tool, but what you do need to know is what is in front of the camera, what is being seen on the monitors, and what is heard or what can be heard when conducting your presentation.

Here are the questions you need to ask the tasker when asked to speak via a videoconferencing platform:

Cameras

- How many are there?
- Are they at all locations?
- Does the camera focused on the speaker follow the speaker if they move from their position either automatically or manually?
- If manually, will there be a person operating the equipment?
- Will the speaker see the audience when speaking?
- Is the live audience being seen by all the distance audiences?
- When a member of the audience asks a question or makes a comment, will a camera be moved toward the person for all else to see?
- Are there multiple monitors displaying both the speaker and other media like slides and videos?
- Are the monitors duplicated at both ends?
- Are the distance end monitors large enough for the audience to see?
- Can microphones be muted? You want microphones in the audi-ence to be muted unless they are asking a question or making a comment.
- Are there microphones available for audience members to be heard when talking?
- What technical support will be available before and during the presentation?

Distance Audience Locations

- How many distance locations are viewing the presentation?
- How many are in each distance location?
- Did they receive any hard-copy handouts that may have been provided to the live audience?
- Are they allowed to ask questions or make comments during the presentation? If not, when?

SPEAKING IN FRONT OF THE WEB CAMERA

Your distance audience is as important as the live one in front of you. Don't only focus on the live audience during the presentation. The camera represents your distance audience. Look straight into the camera on occasion to give the nonverbal cue to the distance audience that you know they are there and are important also. Do not focus on any one person in either audience location. Don't touch your face. The camera may be focused on close shots that only include your shoulders and head. That may not be pretty.

THE CAMERA IS YOUR AUDIENCE: SPEAK TO THEM

The audience watching and listening to you in a video conference is a captive one – and that, as they say, is a good thing. They can only be in one place, and it's your job to direct their gaze to the one place you're in. This analogy of theater vs. film explains it well: When you sit watching a play, you can look wherever you like to observe what's going on: at the actor who's speaking, at his fellow performers, the scenery, or even up at the stage lights. When you watch a film, however, your gaze is captive – you can only look where the camera wants you to look.

If you want to influence your audience in a virtual meeting, you have to look at the camera, not at anyone on another screen. This takes some getting used to. In a recent telepresence training session with a client who was located in another room, he never seemed to look at the audience once – he was always looking over to the side. The reason was that he was looking at me, and I happened to be at the side of the conference room I was in, videotaping.

When we watched the recording, it was immediately obvious that he was looking in the wrong place, and not appearing to speak to his listeners at all. It was an easy fix to get him to direct his gaze at the camera. Teach yourself that the camera IS the audience that you're talking to. Once you get your gaze right, you'll come through as warm and genuine and speaking to your co-attendees. In our second taping in my client session, the difference was positive and dramatic.[3]

There are times when the speaker is only presenting to the live audience in the room. Distance audiences may be included for viewing only and not for participation. If that is the case, the speaker should make that clear to everyone, so there is no misunderstanding on anyone's part.

A negative aspect of telepresence speaking is that no matter what the speaker is doing in the live space, the distance audience has one thing to be looking at, and that is the monitor or projector screen. It becomes memorizing to the point that they tune out and quickly lose concentration. The speaker needs to consider that and take every opportunity to grab the audience's attention using their voice and nonverbal body language. More about that in the next chapter.

CHAPTER REVIEW REFLECTION TOOLS

1. Determine how the room will be set up for your presentation.
2. Determine where the A/V equipment will be set up in the room.
3. A speaker stands on a podium and stands behind a lectern.
4. The projection screen should be close to where the speaker will be standing on the podium.
5. Test the lighting in the room. More light is better than less light. You want to see the whites of the eyes of the audience sitting in the back of the room.
6. When using a microphone, always speak into it and don't let your head move away from it.
7. Always ask to have a wireless microphone to use when speaking. It allows you to move around.
8. Always know what the audience is viewing on their monitor or screen when delivering a presentation via video teleconferencing.

NOTES

1. Projector Screen Size Calculator, www.projectorscreen.com/projector-screen-calculators.
2. Examples of telecommunications applications are Skype, Zoom, WebEx, BlueJeans, AnyMeeting, and RingCentral.
3. Gary Genard, "Speak for Success! Video Conferencing: How to Speak Dynamically in Front of the Camera," December 3, 2017, www.genard-method.com/blog/video-conferencing-how-to-speak-dynamically-in-front-of-the-camera.

7

Delivery Techniques

INTRODUCTION

Chapter 7 includes all the activities that should be taken during the planning stage and throughout the presentation to satisfy what Aristotle meant when he said, "It is not enough to know what to say; one must also know how to say it." This chapter begins with how to introduce both the speaker and the topic to be presented. Then moves on to a discussion on how to get the audience's attention, handling of questions, managing distractions, use of humor, using nonverbal communication, use of your voice as a form of communications, and the speaker's physical appearance. Aristotle's use of "storytelling" is presented as a methodology for clarifying difficult concepts and ensuring "understanding." Finally, methods for how best to summarize material at the conclusion of the presentation.

INTRODUCING THE TOPIC AND SPEAKER

Before the day of your presentation, your potential audience should be notified of your presentation and that you are the speaker. During pre-delivery preparation, you should be providing the tasker with not only the title of your presentation but also a brief abstract that highlights your speech. The abstract should include the objectives and a summary of your presentation and a short biography of you, the speaker. Encourage your tasker to use this information. On too many occasions, I have experienced this not being done. Giving your audience the title and the speaker's name only, tells them nothing. You want to prepare your audience to know what to expect. On many occasions what information the audience has upfront will be the deciding factor on whether they will show up to hear you. Taskers tend not to recognize the importance of this activity, so you need to do that for them. Why? Because you are the one who will be up on the podium, not the tasker. It is up to you to make this happen if you are in a position to do so.

Now, on the day of the presentation, you need to find out from the tasker who will be introducing you and your topic. Don't be surprised if they say no one. They may simply ask you to go up to the podium and begin. Either way, the following remarks should be included in the introduction of your presentation:

Speaker/Topic Introduction Comments

- The speaker's formal name, title, and organization.
- An expanded title of the speech.
- Why the presentation is vital to hear, and how it will make a difference for the audience.
- What is the speaker's experience related to the subject?
- The significant academic/training credentials the speaker has that relate to the subject.
- Significant honors/awards/accomplishments that relate to the speaker's credibility.
- Security Classification of the presentation, if applicable. (This relates to presentations that are classified and require a clearance to be heard.)

PROVIDING SPEAKER BIOGRAPHICAL INFORMATION FOR THE INTRODUCTION

As discussed earlier, the introduction portion of your presentation is vital for setting a strong foundation for the speaker to grab the audience's attention and begin their speech. So let's discuss how to prepare for the introduction.

All speakers should have a resume and/or curriculum vitae (CV), but they don't always have a biography (bio). A résumé (or resume) is a document created by a person to present their background, skills, and accomplishments. Résumés are used for a variety of reasons, but most often they are used to obtain employment. A typical résumé should only be one page, but some are more, containing a "summary" of relevant job experience and education. A CV includes a great deal of life experience and accomplishments, including education, original research, presentations delivered, and papers or books published. Résumés and CVs tend not to be helpful for someone who is about to introduce you when speaking.

A bio is best for this occasion. A bio is not a book or anything like that. It is a one-page bulleted document that highlights key areas of your background and experience. It will give the person introducing you with some content to pull from when they are preparing your introduction. A bio should contain the following information:

Sample Biography

Full name
Email and phone numbers
Website if you have one
Headshot photo (optional)

- Highlight who you are. Example: "An educator, author, consultant, and public speaker."
- If retired, when and with what agency/company.
- Present employer, if related to the topic. If not, optional.
- Key positions in your employment that relate to the topic. If not, optional.
- Essential skills, as related to the topic.
- Academic education or training if related to the topic.
- Awards received if related to the topic. For example, if you were an Eagle Scout, the only time that may be useful for the audience to know is if your topic was on leadership or young adult activities. Military service medals are not necessary to mention, again unless any one of the medals is associated with the topic.
- Books, research, journal articles, etc., written or participated in are excellent if they have something to do with the topic.

When writing your bio or when asked to provide bio information, don't be modest. Be proud of your accomplishments. Your audience needs to know who you are so they can decide whether to believe what you will be saying to them.

The person introducing you should not read your bio verbatim. They can read their short rendition of what they have decided to say, but make sure they don't read everything you wrote. That is a real turn off for the audience, and they stop listening after the third sentence.

I remember when I began hitting the speaker circuit and was asked to provide a bio. I didn't have one prepared, so I decided one day to do just that. After I wrote it, I asked my lovely wife to review it for me. I remember her response after reading it, "Oh my god, you are so full of yourself." I quickly returned a response saying, "Excuse me, I was just asking for you to review it for typos and grammar, not for editorial comments thank you." So again, don't be modest. A bio should contain facts, not opinion, so don't be afraid to list information like that in your bio if it applies.

Your audience wants to know who you are and how much experience you have. Dale Carnegie, who was an American writer and lecturer, and the developer of famous courses in self-improvement, salesmanship, corporate training, public speaking, and interpersonal skills, said it best: "Speakers who talk about what life has taught them never fail to keep the attention of their listeners."[1] That goes back to Aristotle's "storytelling," a technique for sharing life's experiences to exemplify concepts being presented.

If you don't happen to have the credentials and experience to deliver the topic you are speaking on, and this will happen to you if it hasn't already, don't freely offer it up to your audience. Don't begin your presentation apologizing for not having the institutional knowledge about your topic. If you get asked what your experience is at some point in your presentation, don't lie. Give a positive response, such as "This is a whole new area for me. I am learning more about it every day and its significance. I am happy to have been asked to give you a global representation of how it works with more to come soon." You are telling your audience between the lines that you are excited about the topic, happy about being involved with it, and that you were asked to present it with the newly acquired knowledge you have. Don't be uncomfortable with that. You are being honest, and as long as you are prepared to offer the content you have, the audience will be with you.

EXPLAINING THE LOGISTICS OF THE PRESENTATION

You are still in the "introduction" phase of the presentation. Before you begin the "body" phase that contains the main content and evidence, you must explain to the audience what is expected of them during the presentation. The introduction is where you provide them with the following:

- How long the presentation will last.
- When the breaks will be and for how long.
- Whether you will be taking questions during the presentation and if so when. If your time is limited and you want to ensure that you have time to present all your prepared material, hold any questions to the end of the presentation.
- Explain what to do with any handouts you may have provided. Audiences want to know.

MOTIVATION TO LISTEN

As the speaker, you want your audience to hear you, understand you, and remember what you have said. The "hearing you" and "understanding you" is the speaker's responsibility. Making sure you have taken the necessary preparation and testing of audio/visual (A/V) equipment will allow you to be heard. Understanding you is based on the speaker's knowledge of the audience, their needs, and expectations. Remember, you want to be *understood*, not just be *clear* when you are presenting. Being understood focuses on your audience. Being clear focuses on yourself. In other words, "clarity" is only a speaker's perception, whereas "understanding" can be perceived by both speaker and audience together.

As a professor, I can motivate my students to want to hear me, understand me, and remember the content of my lectures by telling them at the introduction of the course that we will have several tests and graded exercises. But what does an audience have to motivate them when they attend a conference presentation, training course, workshop, seminar, or lunch or dinner meeting. Answer: usually nothing. That is where my "Reflections Assignment" can be used to engage the audience, give them a responsibility during the process, make them want to listen, and, finally, provide you, the speaker, with positive summary feedback.

Introduce the "Reflections Assignment" right at the beginning during the introductory phase. To motivate them to complete this assignment, provide each participant with a handout similar to Figure 7.1. That way, all they have to do is fill it out during the presentation. You explain to the audience that "reflections" are bits of knowledge, information, or skills obtained during a learning event that will be personally valuable to them in the future. You continue to tell the audience that they have this

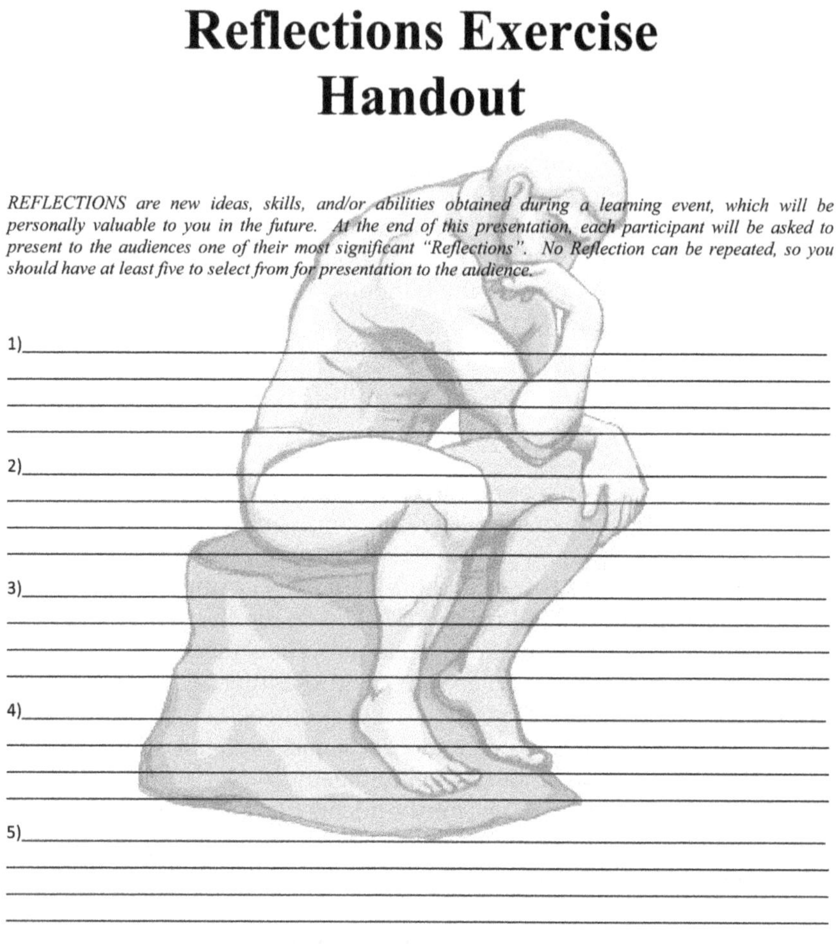

Reflections Exercise
Handout

REFLECTIONS are new ideas, skills, and/or abilities obtained during a learning event, which will be personally valuable to you in the future. At the end of this presentation, each participant will be asked to present to the audiences one of their most significant "Reflections". No Reflection can be repeated, so you should have at least five to select from for presentation to the audience.

1)_____

2)_____

3)_____

4)_____

5)_____

Figure 7.1   Reflections exercise handout sheet. (From Shutterstock.)

assignment to be completed during the presentation. The task is for them to write down a minimum of three reflections that they hear during your presentation and for them to be prepared to discuss one of them during the last segment of the presentation's summary phase. Let them know that you only want to hear a reflection one time, so as audience volunteers are sharing their reflections, if they hear one of their reflections shared, they must have others ready to present. That encourages participants to volunteer at the beginning. The longer they wait to volunteer, the more difficult it becomes to come up with a reflection that hasn't already been mentioned.

You will not believe what happens. No one wants to be left speechless. Everyone in the audience wants to sound intelligent when it is time for them to share their reflection, so they immediately begin paying attention to you the speaker, and they start writing down nuggets of information contained in the presentation. This exercise does several things for the speaker. It keeps most of the audience focused on the topic. They tend to look for items to list on their reflection sheet that will not be used by anyone else. When the speaker is asking for volunteers at the end of the presentation, everyone wants to go first to have their reflection heard before someone else uses it. Finally, the reflection exercise acts as the summary for the speaker because the audience is sharing the significant pieces of information they got from the presentation. It is a win-win experience for both sides.

The Reflections Assignment can only be used on specific types of presentations, but whenever you can use it, you will be glad you did. The reflection exercise becomes the summation of your presentation by telling you the speaker what was the most significant nuggets of information they took away from your presentation.

GETTING AUDIENCE ATTENTION: CREATING A STRONG OPENING STATEMENT

For those of you who have experienced the miracle of childbirth either as a child bearer or an observer, you witnessed the newborn baby's first public speaking experience. The baby was not afraid to cry and scream before your very eyes and ears. The baby grabbed your attention immediately, and you wanted to listen whether it was your child, grandchild, or a dear friend. We learn two things from this experience. First, we are not born afraid to speak in public, we learn to be afraid; and, second, the first cry we experienced was as memorable as if it occurred yesterday. We will discuss being afraid to speak in public later. Right now, we will focus on how to grab the attention of our audience when we first meet them on the podium.

Do not begin your presentation by repeating what has already been said by the person who has introduced you, or by asking the audience, "Can you hear me? Testing, one, two, three. Ah, how much time do I have?" That will turn your audience off quickly, and they will turn to

115

their cell phones to see what is new on Facebook. There are four ways to connect with your audience when you start your speech so you can grab their attention. Any one of the following can be used, reminded that you want to grab and hold their attention throughout your presentation:

1. Ask the audience a rhetorical question, a question to make a point rather than to get an answer.
   Examples:
   - "What is the one piece of physical evidence that can be found in every single crime scene, no matter what the circumstance?" The answer, by the way, is not fingerprints or DNA. It is footwear prints. That would be an excellent question to start with if you were going to discuss the significance of footwear evidence and new technologies used to identify footwear. Most crime scene investigators tend not to focus on shoeprints unless requested.
   - "In criminal law, the intention is one of the mental states (*mens rea*). Can anyone tell me the difference between intention and motive?" This may be an excellent question to start with when the audience is criminal justice professionals, not lawyers.
   - "Can anyone tell me what happened in 1966 that changed the way we look at crime scenes?" The answer is the *US v. Miranda* decision that established the requirement to advise detainees that they have a right to remain silent. One may believe that it was this decision that placed a new emphasis on physical evidence and a decrease of confessions that were relied upon until this decision.
2. Introduce an interesting factoid statement that shocks the audience, or at least makes them think about what will come next.
   Examples:
   - "Since 1989, there have been 2,513 exonerations of innocent criminal defendants in the United States.[2] So somebody has been making mistakes."
   - "Approximately 40% of the forensic science technology viewed on CSI-type TV shows don't exist. So let's talk about how that affects the perception of forensic sciences capabilities."
   - "I define our jury system as 12 people who weren't smart enough to get out of jury duty. These same 12 people are the ones who decide guilt or innocence."
3. Tell a story from your own life that related to your presentation and why the topic of your presentation is essential to the

audience. Reflect on the times you have told a child a bedtime story. You begin with, "Once upon a time…" That immediately gets the child's attention. For an adult audience, you can start by saying, "Let me tell you about what happened to me when…"

If you don't use stories, audience members may enjoy your speech, but there is no chance they'll remember it.

– Andrii Sedniev[3]

Examples:
- "I remember my very first lecture. It was an Introduction to Criminal Justice class to a lecture hall full of freshmen students. There was nothing I would tell them that they wouldn't believe. They were young and impressionable. The subject was so basic; there was no pressure on my part as I began lecturing. About 20 minutes into the lecture, one of the students fell asleep, out cold, gone with the wind. He was a head bobber, with his head moving in circles and falling forward. He was becoming a distraction to others in the class. He became more interesting and entertaining than me, so I pointed to the student next to him and asked him to wake up the student. The student turned to me and said, 'You wake him up, you put him to sleep.' This is a humorous story that didn't happen, but the audience tends to believe it did. I go on to tell the audience that I'm glad that this happened at the beginning of my speaking career, so I could learn that knowing my subject is not enough to be successful as a speaker."
- "I remember the first rape case I investigated. Back then, the primary investigator had to process their crime scenes, so when I left the victim at the hospital after undergoing a medical-legal examination, I responded to the rape scene to process the scene and recover evidence. I was new, and I was the only investigator on duty that weekend. I found biological fluid on the sofa where the victim stated the assault occurred. I cut out a portion of the upholstered material where I found what appeared to be semen. I carefully placed the damp material in a plastic bag to be sent to the crime lab. Later, I found out from the lab technicians that I destroyed the biological evidence by placing it in a plastic bag. I should have air-dried it first and then placed it in a paper bag that could breathe. That is how I learned what not to do at a crime scene."

117

4. Use a quote from a famous person in the field related to the topic. Marlene Dietrich (1901–1992), a well-known American actress, once said, "I love quotations because it is a joy to find thoughts one might have, beautifully expressed with much authority by someone recognized wiser than oneself."[4] Quotations are a great way to begin a speech. They have so much authority because someone else said it, not you, and whatever the quote, the audience immediately believes it. I use famous quotes both in speeches and in my writing.

CREATING A "STAGE EFFECT"

What you are trying to do right at the onset of your presentation is to create what a theatrical professional would define as a "stage effect," which is an emotional event for attracting attention. It doesn't always have to be with words. For example, Ray Semko is a security educator and a professional public speaker who is internationally known for his popular and motivating D*I*C*E security awareness briefings. He has been presenting his D*I*C*E briefings to American audiences for over 30 years, *using props, and wearing costumes and unusual tuxedos* that shock his audiences when he is first introduced to approach the podium. The audience is usually prepared to receive the typical, boring, security awareness briefing required each year, but when they unexpectedly see Semko enter the room, they are captivated by his very presence. His appearance has captured their attention, and what he says is always remembered (Figures 7.2 and 7.3).

SPEAKER MOVEMENT AT THE PODIUM

The speaker should move around and not stand in one place for too long. Movement by the speaker allows the audience to keep their attention on you and not be mesmerized by being focused on one thing only. Move away from the lectern. Move away from the projection screen when you are not discussing content on any particular slide. Get down on the floor level with your audience and move up the aisles if there are any. The additional benefit for the speaker is if you move and members of the audience don't move with you, you know you have a problem with their attention. They are not paying attention, so you need to work harder in that regard.

Figure 7.2 Ray Semko. (Photo and graphic by Cynthia J. Kwitchoff, CJK Creative, with permission by Ray Semko: The D*I*C*E Man.) (See https://www.facebook.com/raysemkodiceman/.)

Figure 7.3 One of the D*I*C*E Man's many tuxedos worn during his presentations. (Photo by Cynthia J. Kwitchoff, CJK Creative, with permission by Ray Semko: The D*I*C*E Man.)

119

What else can you do? Raise your voice or make a physical gesture to emphasize a word or comment you are making. It is the speaker's responsibility to keep the audience engaged, not the audience's. The speaker should have control and be the center of attention. Many of my colleagues in the academic world would not agree with me here, but I believe it is the speaker's job to do anything and everything to hold the audience's attention. After all, it is hard for any human being to sit in one position for an extended period of time. That is why it is crucial to take a break when you get over the 60-minute mark.

ENTERTAINING THE AUDIENCE

It doesn't matter how serious the topic, the prominence of the audience, or the sanctity of the venue where you are speaking, you must be entertaining your audience while you are speaking. By entertaining, I don't mean singing a song and doing a dance on the podium; I mean holding their attention, so they are interested and want to keep listening. For example, Hollywood is in the entertainment business, so let's use one of the movies it produced that will make this point. How many of you readers paid good money at the movie theater to view the film *Titanic*, a 1997 American epic romance and disaster film? It was directed, written, coproduced, and coedited by James Cameron, with starring roles by Leonardo DiCaprio and Kate Winslet. How many readers enjoyed the movie so much that they watched it more than once either back at the theater or on cable or maybe bought the DVD? "This movie, created in 1997, has been around for 20 years. In these two decades, it held the record for box office gross sales for twelve years. When released to DVD in 1999, it became the best-selling DVD and first ever to sell one million copies. As of September 2017, it still holds positions three and two for Top 100 movies of All-Time for Domestic (US) sales and Top 100 movies All-Time Worldwide Gross Sales."[5] The plot to the movie is about the *Titanic* hitting an iceberg and over 1,500 people drowning. Millions of people were obviously entertained by watching this death and destruction. Why? How could this movie be entertaining? Hollywood knows how to do this because it is in the entertainment business. Moviemakers took the historical event and added music and romance to it. "My Heart Will Go On," sung by Céline Dion, has sold over 18 million copies. The romantic relationship and the music softened the death and destruction enough for millions of people to want to watch and listen. Speakers need to do the same, even if they are delivering a eulogy.

USE OF HUMOR

Once you get people laughing, they're listening and you can tell them almost anything.

– Herbert Gardner[6]

I am talking about humor, not joke-telling. There is nothing worse than hearing a speaker tell a joke that has nothing to do with the topic at hand. It becomes nothing but a waste of valuable time, even if the joke is funny. Humor, on the other hand, is the ability to be amusing, expressed in oral communications. A well-known American comedian, actor, singer, and writer, George Burns, once characterized the difference between a comedian and a humorist. He said, "Someone who makes you laugh is a comedian ... Someone who makes you think and then laugh is a humorist."[7] A humorous story that relates to an issue being discussed will balance effectively into a speech. It helps the speaker be liked by the audience and at the same time, be entertaining. It can be used as an icebreaker at the beginning of a speech and then used sporadically throughout the speech to keep the audience's attention. But don't overdo it. You don't want any delivery technique you are using to overshadow the objectives of your speech. Too much of anything is too much.

Ross Shafer, a comedian and motivational public speaker, shares several humorous opening lines and icebreakers for speakers. Here are just a few:[8]

"Thank you. You know, coming here tonight my (husband)(wife) said, 'Whatever you do, don't try to be too charming, witty or intellectual ... just be yourself.'"
"I was told to be accurate. No matter how long it takes."
"Don't you think it's amazing that 200 of us had dinner together and we all pretty much ordered the same thing?"
After a long, tedious introduction delivered by a person introducing you, you could say:

"I guess he (she) decided not to mention my Nobel Prize!"

One of my childhood favorite actors, Groucho Marx, on numerous occasions, would open with, "Before I speak, I have something important to say." What is important to remember when integrating humor is to let the humorous story blend into the content of your speech and not let it be separate and distinct from it. That is the difference between telling a joke and using good humor. There was a time before the internet when speakers had to purchase books on quotable quotes and humorous quotes and stories to

121

integrate into their speeches. I, for one, had purchased more than 20 books that I would refer to when preparing a speech, lecture, or briefing. With the advent of the internet, that is no longer necessary. You can quickly do an internet search for any subject, event, and date and time you need to use.

USE OF HISTORICAL EVENTS

An excellent technique for grabbing an audience's attention and demonstrating the significance of a speech topic is when developing your speech, determine the exact date you will be delivering your speech, and see if anything significant happened on that same month or day. For example, let's say that you are delivering a speech on the Bill of Rights, and you will be delivering the speech in June of that year. Let's say you were going to give it on June 13 of that year. You could begin your speech by reminding the audience that it was June 13, and did anyone know the significance of that date in 1966. The answer is on June 13, 1966, the *Miranda v. Arizona* case was decided by the US Supreme Court that resulted in a ruling that specified a code of conduct for police interrogations of criminal suspects held in custody. The Miranda rights to counsel and the right to remain silent are derived from the self-incrimination clause of the Fifth Amendment. The older members of the audience will be impressed that you knew that date off the top of your head, but the younger members will have assumed you just Googled it. Either way, the historical event will focus on the audience and get their attention.

One way to find some content in this regard is to go to the cable network History Channel's website and click on the tab "This Day in History."[9] That will bring you to a page that lists all the significant events in history that occurred in the present day. The events are broken up into various categories such as wars, sports, crime, art, literature, film history, inventions, and science. To provide you with the same information on the day of your speech, click on the arrow next to the present date, then a drop-down window will show the entire month. There you can go to any month and day of the year, click on it, and view all the events that the History Channel has to offer.

THE POWER OF MOTIVATION, INSPIRATION, AND ENTHUSIASM

Motivation, inspiration, and enthusiasm – these three human behaviors will always coincide with a successful presentation. They relate to the speaker's ability to be believable, passionate, knowledgeable, and caring. When the speaker exhibits these human charateristics in their delivery, the audience will listen. The audience cannot help but sense those same feelings. There are times when you are not motivated, inspired, or enthusiastic about what you are presenting. That is not the audience's fault, nor do they want to hear any excuses from you for your lack of positive emotion. They don't care if you are not feeling well, or if you are not prepared because of a lack of sleep or knowledge of the subject. They deserve your best no matter what your reason for being less.

There was a time when I had a member of my staff presenting security awareness presentations on a full-time basis. Each year we videotaped him doing his presentation in front of a broad audience, approximately 250-plus in attendance. We then would distribute ten thousand DVDs of the presentation to our customers worldwide. On the day of this particular year, when we were going to tape his presentation, he fell on a sheet of ice just outside of the building where the auditorium was located. He came limping into the hall and told me what happened. I asked him if he was bleeding or had broken any bones. He said, "No, I don't think so." I said, "Good, then be ready to go on stage in a few minutes." I also told him, "The live audience in the auditorium and the 10 thousand customers who will be receiving the DVD of his presentation don't care that you fell on the ice, and they certainly don't want to hear you crying about it, so do not even mention it during the videotaping of the presentation. We are producing ten thousand copies of this presentation for mass distribution, and it needs to be your best performance." To this day, he reminds me of this incident, and what he characterizes kiddingly as my total disregard for his well-being. We joke about it because he is a true professional speaker who knows what is important in these situations. After his 90-minute presentation, he wobbled home (a three-hour drive), cried to his wife that he was in pain, and tended to his minor injury.

I guess you could say the staff person in the preceding story was willing to "Win one for the Gipper,"[10] a famous line used as a political slogan by Ronald Reagan.

If you are ever giving a speech about someone or something that "made a difference," there is a beautiful parable titled "The Starfish

Story" that you can use that grabs your audience's attention and heart. Here it is:

THE STARFISH STORY*

One day, an old man was walking along a beach that was littered with thousands of starfish that had been washed ashore by the high tide. As he walked, he came upon a young boy who was eagerly throwing the starfish back into the ocean, one by one.

Puzzled, the man looked at the boy and asked what he was doing. Without looking up from his task, the boy simply replied, "I'm saving these starfish, Sir."

The old man chuckled aloud, "Son, there are thousands of starfish and only one of you. What difference can you make?"

The boy picked up a starfish, gently tossed it into the water, and turning to the man, and said, "I made a difference to that one!"[11] (Figure 7.4)

Figure 7.4 The starfish story. (From Shutterstock.)

---

* This parable has many versions to it where the roles of the old man and the young boy are reversed, so it's the young boy that is asking the question to the old man, or the young boy is a young girl.

124

USE OF NONVERBAL COMMUNICATIONS

Peter Drucker, an American author and management consultant, said it best when he stated, "The most important thing in communication is hearing what isn't said."[12] Many researchers have determined that approximately 60% of communication is nonverbal.[13] Others, like Professor Albert Mehrabian, in his 1971 published book *Silent Messages*, combined the statistical results of the two studies and came up with the now-famous – and famously misused – rule that communication is only 7% verbal and 93% nonverbal. The nonverbal component was made up of body language (55%) and tone of voice (38%), referred to as the 7% rule.[14] It has been my experience that 60% of communications being nonverbal is about right. The real message here is that we need to spend time discussing how nonverbal communications work in the public speaking arena. We can define nonverbal communications in the simplest way as anything the audience can see and the sounds they can hear on the podium during a presentation – before, during, and after. The speaker communicates emotions, attitudes, intentions, demeanor, values, and expressions of importance that the speaker uses to complete the message being delivered. In a courtroom setting, the use of demonstrative evidence in the form of physical evidence exhibits shows the triers of fact certain conclusions made by experts who examined the crime scene and forensic evidence collected, which are other examples of nonverbal communications.

Let's begin with the fundamental nonverbal expressions that all speakers need to be aware of when they are speaking.

Facial Expressions

Facial expressions are transmitted and received simultaneously by the speaker and the audience participants. Criminal investigators and polygraph examiners receive specialized training in this area of study to help them determine their interview subject's truth from lies. Attorneys value facial expressions during jury selection and evaluating juror's expressions when hearing witness testimony. Paul Ekman, Ph.D., calls these facial expressions "microexpressions" that are "facial expressions that occur within a fraction of a second. This involuntary emotional leakage exposes a person's true emotions."[15] The study of microexpressions goes beyond the intent of this book, so we will focus on how we evaluate facial expressions as a speaker to better communicate to our audiences and to better decode what our audiences may be telling us.

125

Facial expressions communicate how we are feeling at that moment, either about the topic we are speaking on or some personal thoughts or physical feelings we are experiencing. Anthropologist Ray Birdwhistell estimated in his research in 1970 that we can make and recognize around 250,000 facial expressions.[16] When I read this, I tried to stand in front of a mirror and count how many different expressions I could make. I stopped shortly after I started. For purposes of public speaking, we will divide facial expressions into nine categories that transmit positive and negative feelings by the audience and speaker while delivering a speech:

- Happiness
- Sadness
- Surprise
- Confusion
- Anger
- Boredom
- Inspiration
- Seriousness
- Excitement

*See if you can identify which facial expression is associated with each numbered photograph (see Figure 7.5). The answers are listed in this chapter's Notes.[17]

Speaker Facial Expressions

You want your facial expressions to parallel the words being spoken to support the content and objectives of your presentation. If nonverbal communication is indeed 60% of what is being received by the audience, then the facial expression is as important as the words you speak. For example, smiling increases the speaker's likeability and attraction, so why wouldn't you be smiling during your presentation? For some speakers, this is something that needs practice. If anyone has ever told you that it is hard for them to know what you are thinking, then you are in that group of speakers who needs practice in this area. Lack of expression is a lack of communication, so practice making the facial expressions listed earlier in a mirror. Even better, practice making facial expressions while practicing a speech.

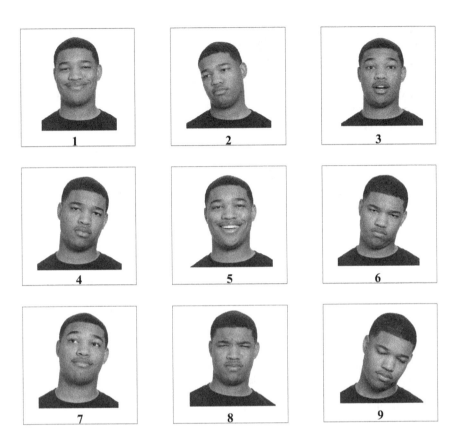

Figure 7.5 Facial expressions. (Photo by Luiz Santos.)

Audience Facial Expressions

Trying to read the facial expressions of your audience can create a positive mindset for the speaker when they are generally smiling and appear to be happy. At the same time, misreading the audience's facial expressions can cause a misinterpretation of what is being communicated by an audience participant. The speaker must realize that while they are speaking, their attention is specifically on what they are saying. On the other hand, audience members can be daydreaming, associating what you are saying with some personal experience, trying to understand what you are saying, or thinking of something else that has nothing to do with what you the speaker is saying. Although the speaker should always be attentive to what the audience is doing, saying, and communicating, sometimes their facial expressions will not be a representation of what they are receiving from you the speaker, but from what they are thinking of in their head at the time. The following Storytelling is two examples that I have experienced in this regard:

I was giving a counterintelligence talk to a group of industrial security officers on the topic of "Operation Security (OPSEC)." The time was shortly after the 9/11 terrorist attacks. I explained how the terrorists used open-source information to be successful that day, causing the deaths of thousands of innocent people. Because the topic was OPSEC, I suggested that if this open-source information was protected, it would have made it more difficult for the terrorists to be successful. Throughout the one-hour presentation I was watching this one particular audience attendee. He was communicating facial expressions that went from seriousness to sadness and finally to anger. Although I was reading his nonverbal communications via his facial expressions correctly, I misread his reasoning. I thought he did not agree with what I was saying or didn't like the presentation, or maybe he didn't like me. When the presentation concluded, he approached me at the lectern. I was ready for the worst, but it was quite different than I expected. He told me throughout my presentation, he was thinking of his cousin, who was one of the victims who lost his life in one of the World Trade Center towers on 9/11. He was listening to what I was saying because he was associating how the use of OPSEC may have made a difference and saved his cousin.

My second story is when I was teaching my Introduction to Criminalistics course. It was early in my teaching career, so the course was 90% traditional lectures. Twice a week for three months, I was watching this one student sitting in the back row every week, communicating the nonverbal facial expression of boredom. I wondered why she never missed class because she always looked so bored. On the last day of the class, I was administering the final examination. While I was sitting at the front of the lecture hall, this same student approached me to hand in her examination paper. She dropped it on the desk, came around the desk toward me and whispered in my ear, "This class was the best class I have ever taken, and I looked forward to coming to class every week. Thank you so much." I totally misread her facial expressions for three months. What I learned that day is everyone expresses their feelings differently, and I should not let any one person in an audience control what I may think is going on with other audience members. People are too complex to be psychoanalyzing them in situations like this.

Eye Contact

Your audience wants to feel that you are talking to them personally, and during your presentation, you want to have eye contact with them. Eye contact conveys a sense of sincerity.

This can only be accomplished in a manageable setting with a certain number of attendees in a room that the speaker can reach. Figure 7.6 is an example of such a manageable setting. The attorney is depicted giving his closing arguments to a jury. He clearly has eye contact with the jury, and as a result, every member of the jury has eye contact with him. There is no question that the attorney has the jury's attention.

Figure 7.6 Two-way eye contact between the attorney and jury during closing arguments. (From Shutterstock.)

Speakers should move around the room to make eye contact with an audience, and when you have made the rounds, you can feel that you have reached everyone at least once. Obviously, in a large conference venue with hundreds of attendees, this is difficult, so the speaker should at least move their head in the direction of each section of the room. Move left to right to center, not in a mechanical motion, but in a natural movement that communicates that you care about everyone in the audience. If you are taking questions or allowing audience participation, look at those persons straight in the eye and recognize them during the exchange of information.

Gestures

Both hand, arm, and body gestures are all very important during a presentation. Gestures can be viewed as subtle or not so subtle cues. We use gestures to take the place of words or help us to increase our understanding of what is being said by the speaker. Some speakers tell me they don't know what to do with their hands. Being an Italian, that has never been a problem for me, so I needed to examine how to help those who stand in front of audiences with their arms by their side like they were at attention. See Figure 7.7, and I will show you.

First, let's find out why and how Italians talk with their hands. Isabella Poggi, a professor of psychology at Roma Tre University (in Rome) and an expert on gestures, has identified around 250 gestures that Italians use in everyday conversation. "There are gestures expressing a threat or a wish or desperation or shame or pride," she said. The only thing differentiating them from sign language is that they are used individually and lack a full syntax, Poggi added.[18] "Sometimes gesturing can get out of hand. Last

Figure 7.7 This series of photographs taken while the author, Tom Mauriello, is delivering a key-note address at the Huntsville, Alabama, Von Braun Center.

130

year, Italy's highest court ruled that a man who inadvertently struck an 80-year-old woman while gesticulating in a piazza in the southern region Puglia was liable for civil damages. 'The public street isn't a living room,' the judges ruled, saying, 'The habit of accompanying a conversation with gestures, while certainly licit, becomes illicit in some contexts.'"[19]

In a study by researchers from the University of Rome, they point out four main reasons hand gestures are important:

1. Hand gestures can help you describe what you're talking about, both literally (e.g., when you talk about drawing a circle, you can motion a circle with your hand) and metaphorically (e.g., you could motion a circle with your hand to say "everybody").
2. Hand gestures can help you point to people and things in your surroundings (e.g., pointing at an object while you say "look at that").
3. Hand gestures can help you add emphasis and structure when you talk (e.g., showing numbers when you count, "1, 2, 3, …").
4. Hand gestures give clues about your emotional state. These gestures are not always connected to what you're saying (e.g., Are you confident? Are you lying? Are you anxious?).

What the study also found is that hand gestures are extremely *reliable*. That is, in general, people seem to agree with what hand gestures mean.[20]

Vanessa Van Edwards, a national bestselling author and behavioral investigator with Science of People, has produced a free training video titled "Master Hand Gestures in 5 Minutes" on her website, which is included in her article "20 Hand Gestures You Should Be Using."[21] For those of you who need some help practicing the use of hand gestures, go to this website and see what they are and how to use them.

Personal Appearance

Personal appearance has to do with what you are wearing and how to look when you are up there on the podium. Clothing and good personal hygiene have the power to influence. I remember complementing an older uniformed police officer who had come into my office when the department had just changed their uniform to an entirely new style and color. When I said to him that he looked pretty sharp in his new uniform, he responded, "When you look good, you *is* good." His nonverbal personal appearance gave a far better impression of him than his choice of verbs. Every speaking situation will dictate a particular type of dress code, from formal, to business, business casual, to casual. The following rules that I

131

list here are general considerations to be made for planning your personal appearance:

1. What will your audience be wearing? Never dress below the audience's dress code.
2. Be well-groomed is consistent with being neat, tidy, and having a pleasing appearance.
3. Is there a dress code requirement that the host organization requires of the speakers? Don't forget that popular film *My Cousin Vinny*, when lawyer Vincent Gambini (Joe Pesci) walked into Judge Chamberlain Haller's (Fred Gwynne) courtroom wearing a leather sports jacket and an open neck collar shirt. The dialogue went like this:

   Judge Haller: What are you wearing?
   Vinny: Huh?
   Judge Haller: What are you wearing?
   Vinny [wearing a leather jacket]: Um, I'm wearing clothes.
   [Judge stares ominously.]
   Vinny: I … I don't get the question.
   Judge Haller: When you come into my court looking like you do. You not only insult me, but you insult the integrity of this court.
   Vinny: I apologize, sir, but, uh … this is how I dress.
   Judge Haller: The next time you appear in my court, you will look lawyerly. And I mean you comb your hair, and wear a suit and tie. And that suit had better be made out of some sort of … cloth. You understand me?
   Vinny: Uh yes. Fine, Judge, fine.

4. Wear conservative colors and clothing designs, clothes that will not stand out and be a distraction.
5. Don't wear loud ties with messages, images, or logos on them.
6. Don't wear professional lapel pins or flashy jewelry. Audience members will be squinting with their eyes trying to figure out what the pin says on it. On several occasions when I use to wear a lapel pin while speaking, I had audience attendees come up to me after my presentation and say something like, "What does your pin say? I have been trying to figure it out for the entire presentation, and couldn't see it." So for my entire presentation, these folks were focused on my lapel pin and what it said, rather than what I was saying. I don't wear lapel pins anymore, and I don't wear rings or watches that tend to stand out.

7. Women need to consider wearing clothing that will allow them to attach a lavalier microphone device on their person. Otherwise, they will find themselves holding the remote unit in one hand and the microphone in the other.

8. No baseball hats. If you need to hide something on the top of your head, wear a more conservative hat.

I was attending a senior leadership training program, and on one occasion, a speaker was introduced as a forensic psychologist, Ph.D. When he came up to the podium, he was wearing a wrinkled plaid suit jacket with elbow pads, a loosely worn necktie, and a baseball cap with a ponytail protruding from the opening in the back of the hat. His appearance was unimpressive and distracting for what was believed to be a professional delivering a professional presentation. His topic was on the subject of how we, as criminal justice professionals, tend to allow our biases to interfere with our good judgment and how we must overcome those biases as we search for the truth. While he was speaking, he casually removed his cap, and with it came the ponytail that was a wig sewn into the back of the hat to look like it was the permanent hair of the subject wearing it. It was all a "stage effect" created by the speaker to make his point associated with his topic. Although I cannot speak for the rest of the attendees, I know that my opinion of the speaker changed dramatically from the time when I first thought he had a real ponytail and he thought his appearance was acceptable, until the time I learned it was a stage effect. Yes, I let my biases interfere with what was, rather than what I thought it should be.

Using Your Voice

The tone of your voice carries as much information as the words you speak. There are five adjustments that you can make with your voice that will communicate volumes of information without selecting any specific words. They are as follows:

1. Volume – First, your baseline volume must always be loud enough to be heard. Remember the three objectives of this book, to be *heard*, *understood*, and *remembered*. You can never be understood and remembered if your audience cannot hear you. If your voice is not strong enough to be carried across the room, then ask for a microphone and use it. Second, a technique for drawing attention

to a specific concept you are presenting is to change from a loud tone of voice to a softer tone of voice when uttering the keywords or phrases. That is a method to bring importance to something that you are saying. The volume variation grabs your audience's attention and makes them listen.

2. Pronunciation of letters and words – This is a difficulty I have had while being brought up and educated in the suburbs of Boston, Massachusetts. Accents can be a distraction to audiences and a challenge for speakers when trying to present valuable content. I only had moved from Massachusetts to Maryland for two years when I began my public speaking career. I was wondering why my audiences were smiling or laughing when I hadn't said anything humorous. I eventually realized it was how I was pronouncing certain words or letters. Although people would always say I love to hear the Boston accent, it was doing nothing for me as a speaker. My accent was a distraction and, in some instances, a source of misunderstanding. It took me five years for my ears to even hear the accent or recognize I had an accent. Most accents in the US are subtle enough not to be an issue, but if you have a strong accent do what you can to eliminate the distraction. You may have noticed that local TV news anchors tend to have regional accents, but when you listen to national news anchors, there is no indication of an accent that is recognizable. Hearing and speech academic departments research dialects and provide training on how to eliminate them. Eliminating accents is certainly not necessary for most public speakers, but professional national speakers find it necessary.

3. Rate or speed in which you say words – How fast or slow you speak certain words or a variation of the two speeds can communicate a certain mood that you may want to project. You may say quickly, "You must place wet or damp biological fluids found at a crime scene in a paper-bag container … each … and … every … time!" Those last four words are stated much slower, adding emphasis or meaning to the entire message.

4. Pauses – Pauses between subheadings of information is another way to include emphasis and meaning to your message.

5. Variety – All four of the above used in a meaningful sporadic manner will dynamically communicate your message as long as

134

you don't overuse any one. Remember, too much of anything is too much.

It is, essentially, a matter of the right management of the voice to express the various emotions – of speaking loudly, softly, or between the two; of the high, low, or intermediate pitch; of the various rhythms that suit various subjects. These are the three things – the volume of sound, modulation of pitch, and rhythm – that a speaker bears in mind.—Aristotle

ASKING AND RECEIVING QUESTIONS

Asking questions can be one of the best ways to engage your audience and keep them actively involved in your presentation. How many times do we hear a speaker ask a question, then there is that awkward silence because no one is raising their hand to answer. Sometimes it may be a rhetorical question, but usually, it is being used by the speaker to try to engage the audience. When no one answers the question, the speaker gets nervous and just answers their own question. Therefore, the intent of using the question to engage the audience has been lost. So what can you do? The answer is simple. Ask the question and then *shut up*! Yes, shut up and give the audience time to understand the question being asked, think of a response to the question, formulate the answer, and think about raising their hand. That takes time. Use a "pause" that we just discussed earlier when using your voice as a method to communicate. How long should you pause? The answer: 10 seconds (counting to yourself one thousand one, one thousand two, etc.) What should you be doing while you are counting? Stare into the eyes of your audience (Figure 7.8).

Don't look away from them. If you do that, you have the audience off the hook to respond. If you stare at them, they become uncomfortable, and you force them to come up with an answer because someone in the audience wants to stop the awkwardness. It works most times. Try it. You will be surprised how well it works. But you have to be strong. You have to stand there looking straight ahead, moving your eyes across the audience. When you finally get a response, thank that participant and tell them how much you appreciate their response. It will help you gain rapport with your audience.

It is best to plan your questions ahead of time during the planning stage of your presentation. That way, you can integrate the audience's responses into your presentation to support your objectives. Distinguish

Figure 7.8   Asking a question. (From Shutterstock.)

the questions you ask to receive "information" or "opinion" type responses. Answers to information questions are either right or wrong. For example, "What is your departmental policy for establishing a chain of custody?" is asking for a specific answer. An example of an opinion question would be, "What do you think is the most common type of physical evidence that can be found in a crime scene?" Make them short and clear, and make sure you relate your questions to the audience's background so they have a frame of reference when attempting to respond.

Finally, at the end of a particular section of your presentation, or after presenting a difficult concept, you may want to ensure that your audience is understanding. Typically, we ask the audience, "Are there any questions?" More times than not, the audience stares at you, and there is no response. Try changing the question to "What are your questions?" The question is now a more positive inquiry, whereas you are suggesting that you understand there are questions, so you are asking your audience to tell you what they are. You have a better change to encourage a response from your audience that way.

When receiving a question from your audience, listen carefully to what the question is, acknowledge and thank them for asking the question, clarify the question by restating it to ensure you got it right, and then answer. If you don't know the answer, say so. It is OK not to know everything.

I recall the first time I was asked a question by one of my students and had no idea what the answer was. Thankfully it occurred during the first semester I began as a teacher. The question had a Latin phrase in it, so I had no idea what the answer could be. I knew this day would come, and I was not prepared for it. It was before the internet, so I couldn't tell the student to "Google it." I had no choice but to tell the truth. That is precisely what I did. I said to the student very sheepishly, "I'm sorry, but I just don't know the answer to your question." The student immediately turned to me, looked straight into my eyes and stated, "That's OK professor, you are not expected to know everything." No one had ever told me that. The pressure that I was experiencing was immediately removed from my shoulders. I thanked the student and promised to get the answer back to her and the rest of the class. The question, by the way, was "What does the Latin term *writ of certiorari* mean?" For those of you who do not know the answer, "a writ of certiorari is an order a higher court issues to review the decision and proceedings in a lower court and determine whether there were any irregularities."[22]

CHAPTER REVIEW REFLECTION TOOLS

1. Provide the tasker with not only the title of your presentation but also a brief abstract of your presentation.
2. Make sure the person who will introduce you has your biography.
3. Tell the audience the logistics of your presentation and what you expect them to do during your speech.
4. Remember, you want to be understood, not just clear when you are presenting. Being understood focuses on your audience. Being clear focuses on yourself.
5. Consider using the "Reflection Exercise" for presentations of two or more hours.
6. Create a strong opening statement for your presentation during the introduction.
7. Use a quote from a famous person in the field related to your topic.

8. Move around the podium. It allows the audience to keep their attention on the speaker.
9. Be entertaining. It will make your audience like you.
10. Use humor, not joke-telling.
11. Too much of any one delivery technique is too much.
12. Use historical events that occurred the same date of your speech.
13. Motivate, inspire, and be enthusiastic during your presentation.
14. Sixty percent of oral communication is nonverbal.
15. Keep good eye contact with your audience.
16. Let your gestures (body language) help you communicate your message.
17. Project your voice.
18. The tone of your voice carries as much information as the words you speak.
19. When asking a question of the audience, ask it, and then shut up.

NOTES

1. "Dale Carnegie Quotes," Quotes.net, www.quotes.net/quote/50221.
2. The National Registry of Exonerations, "Our Mission," www.law.umich.edu/special/exoneration/Pages/mission.aspx (accessed November 2019).
3. Andrii Sedniev, MBA, is the founder of the Magic of Public Speaking system which has helped hundreds of speakers worldwide.
4. "Marlene Dietrich Quotes," www.brainyquote.com/quotes/marlene_dietrich_161854.
5. Jillian Zimmerman, "Why Is Titanic the Most Watched Movie of All Time?" October 2, 2017, https://blogs.cisco.com/customerstories/why-is-titanic-the-most-watched-movie-of-all-time.
6. Herbert George Gardner (December 28, 1934–September 25, 2003), better known as Herb Gardner, was an American commercial artist, cartoonist, playwright and screenwriter.
7. George Burns, "Quotable Quotes," *Readers Digest*, September 1976.
8. Ross Shafer, "Opening Lines & Ice Breakers for Speakers," http://rossshafer.com/wp-content/uploads/2015/09/Good-Opening-Lines.pdf.
9. "This Day In History" History.com, www.history.com/this-day-in-history.
10. The line is taken from the 1940 Warner Bros. movie *Knute Rockne, All American*, which tells the story of Knute Rockne, Notre Dame football coach, which starred Pat O'Brien portraying the role of Rockne and Ronald Reagan as player George Gipp.
11. "The Parable," Starfish Project, https://starfishproject.com/the-parable/.
12. Peter Drucker (1909–2005) was a renowned American author and consultant in the field of organizational development and management, and invented the concept of Management by Objectives (MBO).

13. According to well-known social anthropologist Edward T. Hall.
14. Philip Yafffe, "The 7% Rule: Fact, Fiction, or Misunderstanding," *Ubiquity*, October 2011, article 1.
15. Paul Ekman Group, "Micro Expressions," www.paulekman.com/resources/micro-expressions/. Also see Ekman's book *Telling Lies: Clues to Deceit in the Marketplace, Politics, and Marriage?*
16. Allan and Barbara Pease, "Fist Chapter: 'The Definitive Book of Body Language,'" *New York Times*, September 24, 2006, www.nytimes.com/2006/09/24/books/chapters/0924-1st-peas.html.
17. The answers for each of the numbered facial expressions are (1) happiness, (2) boredom, (3) surprise, (4) seriousness, (5) excitement, (6) anger, (7) inspiration, (8) confusion, (9) sadness.
18. Rachel Donadio, "Rome Journal: When Italians Chat, Hands and Fingers Do the Talking," *New York Times*, June 30, 2013, www.nytimes.com/2013/07/01/world/europe/when-italians-chat-hands-and-fingers-do-the-talking.html?_r=0.
19. Ibid.
20. "How to Use Hand Gestures in a Powerful Way When You Communicate," March 16, 2018, https://socialtriggers.com/21-hand-gestures-for-powerful-communication/; Fridanna Maricchiolo, Augusto Gnisci, and Marino Bonaiuto, "Hand Gestures in Speech: Studies of Their Roles in Social Interaction," ResearchGate, January 2005, www.researchgate.net/publication/239586939_Hand_gestures_in_speech_studies_of_their_roles_in_social_interaction.
21. Vanessa Van Edwards, "20 Hand Gestures You Should Be Using," Science of People, www.scienceofpeople.com/hand-gestures/.
22. USLegal.com, "Writ of Certiorari Law and Legal Definition," https://definitions.uslegal.com/w/writ-of-certiorari/.

Part II

Special Criminal Justice and Forensic Sciences Presentation Tasks

Chapters in Part II address the oral communications categories of activities that a criminal justice professional may encounter. Chapters include advice and guidance for the criminal justice professional on how to apply the skills discussed in Part I to the oral communications activities that a criminal justice professional or any professional may experience. They include academic teaching and guest lecturing, training courses and workshops, media interviews, TV documentary show on-camera dialogues, police–community relations presentations in the community, plenary and scientific talks in conference-type settings, and courtroom expert testimony.

8

Presentation Categories Related to the Criminal Justice Sciences

INTRODUCTION

Chapter 8 lists each criminal justice-related presentation into the following general categories: informational, scientific or technical, motivational and inspirational, persuasive, testimonial, training and educational, and impromptu and extemporaneous discussions, and how to plan and prepare a presentation for each. The chapter includes specific discussions in criminal justice and forensic science type presentations such as police–community relations sessions at town hall events, scientific paper presentations at professional association meetings, panel discussions, expert and congressional testimony, keynote and plenary sessions, and lectures and workshops.

Speakers are asked to present talks to audiences that either expect to hear information specific to their interest or need, or they are part of a group that is present in an audience for other organizational requirements. The programs may be educational or training. Having a speaker on the agenda is what is always included in these programs. Sometimes the speaker is given a specific topic to cover, sometimes not. Whatever circumstance arises, the speaker must first know whether the speech is intended to be informational, inspirational, motivational, persuasive, or direct testimonial. Each of these intended speeches falls into several criminal justice–related presentations that are covered in this chapter.

INFORMATIONAL

Whether the topic is given to you or you are asked to choose the topic, you need to refer back to Chapters 1, 2, and 3 to begin planning your speech. How much time do you have? What does the audience know about the topic? How many attendees will be in attendance? Does the topic relate to the theme of the overall program? What does the audience want to walk away with after the presentation? Is the audience expected to do something with the information presented? The tasker should provide answers to these questions. Informational presentations may become persuasive, and all presentations should be motivational. You may be demonstrating some new technology or process. Whatever it is, know exactly what its purpose is so you can begin preparing your speech.

Police–Community Relations Speeches

Police–community relations speeches at town hall and community events are wonderful examples of informational speeches. The idea of having the police go out to the community and discuss criminal activity or crime prevention talks, only motivates audiences to come and listen if there is a problem. It has been my experience that if you go out to the community to give a crime prevention talk in an area of the community where they have not had a crime problem, no one shows up. But if you go back to that same community after a rape, robbery, or burglary has occurred in the neighborhood, everyone wants to hear from the police to get answers to who, what, where, and why it happened. The community in this situation wants to hear from you in this informational style presentation: (Figure 8.1)

- What is your objective in speaking to them on this day? Are you looking for help to solve some crime? Are you just wanting to provide them with information about the crime? Have you been asked to speak on this crime by the community?
- What happened? (Unless the information needs protection for investigation purposes.)
- Is there any description of suspects? If so, what are they?
- What information is the police looking for from the community that can help them solve the criminal activity?
- How are the police going to solve the criminal activity? Are they doing something different to solve the crime?
- What can citizens do to prevent this from happening in the future?

144

Figure 8.1 Police chief speaking during a town hall meeting. (From Shutterstock.)

- How will you persuade the audience that everything is being done by the police to solve the issue?
- Is there any statistical data available to strengthen your content? For example, provide the audience with the crime statistics for the audience's neighborhood, to provide factual data on how significant the crime issue is or is not.
- Ask the audience to hold questions and comments until the end of the presentation. Ensure the audience you will take all questions and comments at the end, but that you want first to present your information. (Audiences will take direction from the speaker if you guide them at the beginning of your speech.)
- If time allows, a demonstration of tactics being used to solve the issue can be a positive message in your address.
- Officers who work in the neighborhood should be present at the presentation to give firsthand information to the audience, and to show they are engaged.
- This event could be confrontational, so prepare to be able to respond in a professional, nonconfrontational manner.

Breakfast, Luncheon, and Dinner Speeches

Breakfast, luncheon, and dinner speeches are the most difficult to deliver. The most obvious reason is that the audience attendees are usually hungry

Figure 8.2 Serving food during a presentation. (From Shutterstock.)

and want to eat. They generally do not want to have to listen to a speaker while they are eating. The second less apparent but essential reason is that it is a time when the attendees want to use this opportunity to network with colleagues or chat in a social atmosphere with colleagues to see how they have been since the last time they met. It is also an opportunity to meet with likeminded people from all different geographical areas who share a common discipline or field, and it is a great way to meet new people in their field. Having a speaker interrupt this opportunity is a mistake sometimes, but that will not change the fact that you are the interrupter. The third reason for this being a challenging venue to speak in is that the food servers are walking around, making noise, asking questions of the attendees while you are talking, and being a general distraction. Even if the attendees eat first before your presentation, that causes the attendees to have to eat quickly, and then when you begin speaking, the food servers start clearing the tables of the glasses, dishes, and utensils walking around all the tables in front of you.

Things to consider during the planning and delivery process when food is being served:

- *Timing.* Determine how and when the meal will be served and when the dishes will be removed. Schedule your presentation when the least amount of food-related activities will be

146

happening. Meet with the food server supervisor and see what you can do to work around this issue. It is my opinion that no one is looking for a long speech at a breakfast, lunch, or dinner event, so I suggest seeing if you can give your address at the very beginning of the event, and make it short and concise. Your audience will love you for it.

- *Seating arrangement*. Round tables require a third of your attendees to have their backs to the speaker. See if the tables can be set to eliminate those positions. It is uncomfortable to have to twist your body one way or the other to view the speaker.
- *Movement*. Because of distractions in the room and the seating positions not always being conducive for viewing, the speaker should move around the room. The change allows each attendee to view the speaker, and for the speaker to practice good eye contact with everyone.
- *Use of audiovisual accompaniment*. Short informative presentations usually do not lend themselves to needing A/V support, but I always encourage its use when applicable. Because the audience doesn't expect A/V usage, they tend to be pleasantly surprised and appreciative. Warning: These types of venues are usually in restaurants and hotels, and requesting A/V equipment for a short period can be costly to the host. If I am going to use A/V in these circumstances, I bring my own A/V equipment. Venues usually have screens available or installed in the room.
- *Objective*. Although most presentations in this type of venue are "informational" in nature, that is not always the case. I was invited to be the guest speaker at a criminal defense attorney's dinner meeting, and the monthly event had two objectives. The first was a networking objective that allowed members to keep in touch with their colleagues. The second was a training or educational purpose. The tasker told me that they looked to the guest speaker to present content that would further their knowledge in some aspect of the criminal justice practice.

Plenary Sessions

Plenary sessions, also referred to as a general session, are presentations delivered at a conference in which all members attending the conference are invited. Most keynote addresses are plenary sessions. They are scheduled when no other events are scheduled, so to get the largest attendance as possible. The event coordinator (tasker) will request from the plenary

147

speaker a topic that focuses on the theme of the conference and will be of interest to all the conference attendees. The plenary session can be as short as 20 minutes and as long as 1 hour. It is a significant part of all trade shows and professional conferences. These meetings are usually held on opening day, although I have experienced some conferences that schedule a plenary session at the beginning of each day of a conference with break-out sessions that follow.

The most effective plenary sessions are those delivered for the benefit of the audiences and the event attendees, not the event organization itself. Their purpose is a combination of engaging the audience, setting the tone for the conference, creating a memorable experience, and, most important, sharing valuable information. They should be upbeat, motivating, and inspirational in tone. The credentials of the speaker should have some dominance in the field, but not necessarily a high-ranking dominance. Many times high-ranking speakers provide no value because they have no experience in the organization they manage. They demonstrate that when reading their speeches written by someone else there is a lack of passion for the words coming out of their mouth. If you are selected as a plenary or keynote speaker, take the opportunity seriously and seek out content to present that will "make a difference" to the audience.

Panel Discussions

Panel discussions are informational events that are a public exchange of ideas, giving experts and audience members the chance to discuss a particular topic. The moderator of a panel discussion is as important as the panel members themselves (Figure 8.3).

Figure 8.3 Discussion panel. (From Shutterstock.)

The moderator's role is as follows:

- Keep the panel small and focused – Make sure that the panel members have different views of the topic in discussion.
- Panel member selection – Select a cross-section of panel members that will ensure all aspects of the topic can be covered. For example, if you are discussing a new forensic technology being used to examine evidence, having a forensic scientist familiar with the technology, an investigator who has used the information obtained from the technology, an evidence technician trained to find and collect the evidence as result of the technology, and an attorney that can discuss the legal implications of the relevance of the evidence, may be excellent panel members to have present.
- Plan the questions ahead of time – Provide the questions to the panel members ahead of time and assign questions evenly among the members.
- Open with a clear definition of the topic being discussed – Ensure that the audience, as well as the panel members, understand the topic and why it is being discussed.
- Introduce the panel members – Having the moderator giving the introduction will allow the moderator the ability to explain why the panel member has been selected. It ensures that the panel member's background, as it relates to the discussion topic, is appropriately stated. On the other hand, having the panel member introduce themselves allows them to establish rapport with the audience as well as be more relaxed with the other panel members. I suggest using the same criteria listed in Chapter 2 for introducing speakers.
- Keep the focus on the panel (not the moderator) – Even if the moderator is familiar with the discussion topic, they should remain in the role of moderator and let the panel do the discussion.
- Control the discussion of individual panel members – Instruct the panel members to provide short answers to your questions. Be prepared to cut off panel members who talk too much. Use a phrase to interrupt the long-winded panel members like, "I understand what you are saying, so let's hear from the other members about how they feel about that same issue."
- Have microphones available for panel members on the podium as well as audience members on the floor who may want to ask a question or make a comment – Being heard is a successful means

to being understood and remembered, so ensure that each panel member has a microphone in front of them and that they used it. Have microphones positioned in the aisles for audience members to ask questions and make comments, or use staff members equipped with handheld microphones to hand to audience attendees who wish to make a statement or ask a question.

The panel member's role is the following:

- Be prepared to make an opening statement – Ask the moderator ahead of time whether they will be asking each panel member to make an opening statement. If so, rather than making an offhand comment, prepare a clear and concise statement. Don't read it, have your statement in bullet form to jog your memory of the critical points you want to make. Key points should be about your knowledge and experience with the topic at issue, your feelings about the subject, and the benefits or problems with the issue being discussed.
- Know who the panel members will be – Try to get a sense of what the other panel members will be adding to the discussion. Having access to each panel member's biography would be helpful. The moderator should have that information available. The last time I was asked to be on a panel discussion, it was at a media conference representing investigative reporters. The topic had to do with forensic sciences, and I can't tell you any more than that because I was not given any further details. After the hour-long discussion was over, I still couldn't tell you what the objective of the discussion was. What I do know was that the panel member sitting next to me was an attorney that I had a significant disagreement with on a related topic that we had done for a nationally syndicated TV news show several years prior.[1] It would have been nice to know that before the panel discussion began.
- Don't be argumentative – You can disagree without being argumentative. The objective of a panel discussion is to present all sides of an issue or topic. You are not in a court of law arguing a case.

Scientific Poster Sessions

A scientific research poster is sometimes referred to as a conference poster because that is where they are usually presented. It is a tool that researchers use to present research data in a structured manner. It is sometimes used instead of a formal lecture if the creator of the poster is uncomfortable performing in front of large audiences. It also allows for one-on-one or small group dialogue with a viewer (audience) receiving immediate feedback. Posters are more commonly used by young scientists who are just beginning their careers and hoping to share their research with interested colleagues.

I find poster sessions to be boring and uneventful. Most posters are full of small text, lack images that grab your attention, and uninviting by many presenters. They are a method for getting relevant research out in a venue that supports a field of study with an opportunity to exchange information in an informal atmosphere to only those who are interested. You can be sure that if someone stops in front of your poster while you are there, they usually are interested and want to hear from you. So be inviting to your potential viewers and express the positive emotions of motivation, inspiration, and enthusiasm (Figure 8.4).

Points to remember when preparing and delivering a poster:[2]

- The three most essential prerequisites for visual images are that they be *carefully prepared*, *simple*, and *necessary in the storyline*.
- Include only images that are necessary to the function within the storyline.

Figure 8.4 Photo of Lead Forensic Artist, Sandra Enslow, Los Angeles County Sheriff's Department, standing next to her scientific poster, "Diligence, Dedication & Devotion: Reaching Back into History for the Image of a Victim." The poster was created and presented by her at the American Academy of Forensic Sciences Poster Session, during the 71st AAFS Annual Scientific Meeting, Baltimore, Maryland, February 18–23, 2019.

- The less busy a figure appears, the more justice it does to the information it attempts to communicate.
- Avoid showing tables, complex equations, or nucleotide and amino acid sequences, if possible.
- A poster should be aesthetic and clean. The layout should be organized in vertical columns rather than as horizontal rows, and displayed items should be numbered to guide the reader through the poster.
- Like any scientific presentation, the poster should *tell a story*. Choose a brief and informative title and provide a concise introduction that indicates why the work presented is important within the context of a major scientific principle. Describe the approach in an engaging, condensed style without excessive detail, and organize the presentation of data in a logical, coherent sequence. The lower portion of the poster should contain a small number of well-phrased conclusions and a major, concise summary statement.
- A poster should include only material relevant to the storyline.
- Remember that it is not the number of people who come to view your poster but the quality of interactions with them that determines its success.

SCIENTIFIC OR TECHNICAL

Scientists and technical people tend to be left-brained thinkers meaning that the left side of their brain is dominant. Left-brainers are mostly analytical and methodical, sometimes to a fault when viewed by a right-brained person who is more creative or artistic in their thinking. Figure 8.5 illustrates how left- and right-brain people see the world and how they communicate. They are very different, which means we have to consider this factor when preparing a scientific or technical presentation. Don't forget that it is not your knowledge and expertise in the subject matter and the content of your presentation that will make your presentation successful. The success of your presentation will be measured by how well you delivered it.

First, the speaker must recognize whether they are a left- or right-brain thinker. If you are preparing a scientific or technical speech, chances are you are left-brained. Next, refer to Part I of this book and consider all the processes laid out in those chapters. For example:

LEFT BRAIN vs RIGHT BRAIN

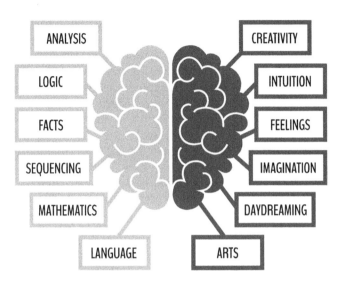

Figure 8.5 A speaker's left brain vs right brain dominance. (From Shutterstock.)

The tasker – Who is asking you to present the speech, and why?

The objective – Determine the presentation objectives and how to relate them to your audience. Are you being asked to educate, train, or inform the audience?

The title – Scientific and technical speech titles can be more interesting than the presentation itself, but mostly the opposite is true. Titles should be a tool to draw your audience's interest. They should be short, concise, understood, and attention-grabbing. Consider the audience when developing your title. The audience will attempt to decode the title in their language, so make it simple.

The audience – Who is your audience? How much do they know about your topic? Determine the depth of your audience's knowledge of the topic. Are they your colleagues who have a baseline knowledge of the topic, or are they right-brainers who only want to receive a strategic view of the topic? Why is the audience coming to hear you? Have they chosen to come to listen to your

presentation, or are they required to come? In a conference setting, audiences are usually there to learn what's new in their field.
Transmitting – This is where the rubber meets the road. Do not forget that visuals like PowerPoint slides should augment the spoken word, not be in place of it. Slides are visuals, so don't be afraid to use images in conjunction with relevant text. Images are easily remembered, where text is not. See Figures 8.6 and 8.7 comparing two PowerPoint slides with the same message. If the presenter is going to recite the words seen in Figure 8.6, then what is the purpose of the slide. Figure 8.7, on the other hand, allows the viewer to hear the speaker talk, while the slide forms a picture in the mind of the viewer. Figure 8.7 will be remembered, and Figure 8.6 will not.

Don't fill your slides with graphs and charts that are meaningless to fill up space on a slide. If you have data that is important to your research, but not crucial to what you are presenting in your speech, then provide handouts with the data, and if the audience members are interested, they will take one and read it later. Today's video projectors and camera systems are so bright and vivid that if you want to demonstrate some technology or scientific experiment in the laboratory, using slides or short video clips do that nicely. Your smartphone has both still photography and video that can do that for you. It is easy to download these items onto your computer and into a PowerPoint program.

Morphology of Hair

- Hair is an appendage of the skin that grows out of an organ known as the hair follicle.

- The length of a hair extends from its root or bulb embedded in the follicle, continues into a shaft, and terminates at a tip end.

- It is the shaft, which is composed of three layers—the cuticle, cortex, and medulla—that is subjected to the most intense examination by the forensic scientist.

Figure 8.6 Both PowerPoint slides depicted in Figures 8.6 and 8.7 communicate the same information. Figure 8.6 is uses text only, and Figure 8.7 uses images only. (Lecture slides created by author, Thomas P. Mauriello.)

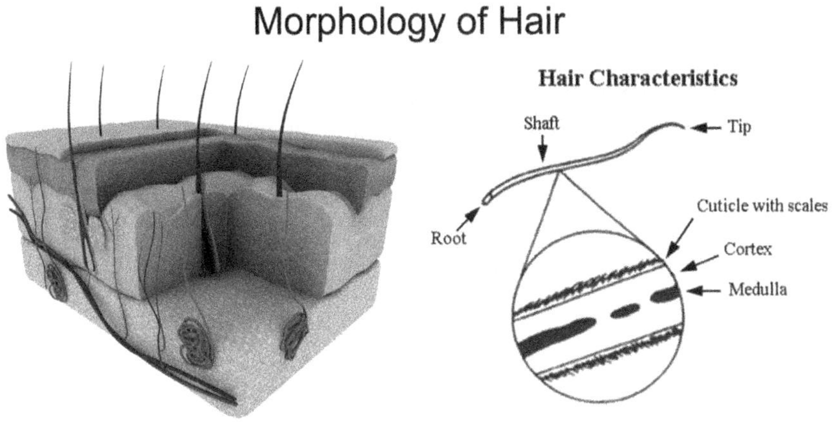

Figure 8.7 PowerPoint slide of images depicting the morphology of a hair follicle. (Lecture slides created by author, Thomas P. Mauriello.)

MOTIVATIONAL AND INSPIRATIONAL

Motivational and inspirational presentations for criminal justice events are are no different then in any other professional career field. They are presented at banquets, promotion and award ceremonies, graduations, town hall meetings, retirements, and eulogies. Sometimes they are time fillers in a more extensive program, or tradition dictates they always have a speaker at a particular event. More times than not, the speaker will be asked to deliver this type of speech with no direction from the tasker. No guidance, no topic, and no help. They will say something like, "Make it motivational to inspire the audience." Having no specific topic requires a lot of planning and questions to be asked of the tasker and prospective attendees.

The following are different settings where motivational and inspirational presentations are delivered. There is certain information that must be obtained during the planning stage of the presentation. I have listed a series of questions that need answers for the speaker to prepare their speech.

155

Banquets

- What is the name of the event?
- Why did you get asked to be the speaker?
- Who does the audience represent, and how many are expected to attend?
- Is an organization tied to the group or the event?
- What other activities will there be at this event? Will there be an agenda handed out to the audience? If so, obtain one. Be aware of all other activities during the event. You don't want surprises.
- What has the group accomplished to merit a banquet?
- How much time will be allowed for your presentation? Don't let the tasker get away with sayings, something like, "Whatever you want." Review the banquet agenda with the tasker and come up with a suitable time limit for the presentation. Generally, 15 to 20 minutes is satisfactory.
- What is the group about, and what activities is it involved with that could be considered inspirational?
- Is there something that the group needs to hear to motivate attendees to do something in the future?

Promotion and Award Ceremonies

- Are you a guest speaker or a presenter for the event?
- If you are a guest speaker, is there a specific topic they want you to cover?
- Will you be asked to present the award(s) or certificate(s), or pin a badge on the promotes or awardees?
- Will you be asked to read a citation that describes the promotion(s) or award(s)?
- Can you get a biography for each of the participants?
- Is there an agenda that will be handed out? If so, obtain one and review it.

Graduations

Consider a theme or topic for the speech that will reflect on the graduates' training and how it will make a difference for them in the field.

- Who are the graduates?
- What career field do the graduates represent?

- Is there a theme associated with the event? If so, what is it, and how can you integrate it into your speech?
- What is the agenda?
- At what point in the graduation exercise will you be delivering your speech?
- Are the graduates all from one organization, or do they represent several agencies?
- Does the leadership of the tasking agency request any specific topic to be presented?
- Did the graduate class have a leader? If so, ask to talk to them to see if something humorous or usual happened during the training that could give you some material for the speech.

Town Hall Meetings

Town hall meetings can be associated with crime prevention, crime control, and crime awareness.

- Were you invited to speak? Were you commanded to speak? Did you invite yourself to speak?
- Will the event be confrontational? If so, determine how you can turn that around and make it a positive experience.
- Have you been asked to have answers to specific questions by the tasker or community? If so, make sure you have whatever information or statistics you can supply as part of your presentation.
- Will you be the only one speaking? Will your senior leadership or local politicians be there to speak also? If so, coordinate with those people to ensure you don't present conflicting information.
- Are you going to be taking questions? If so, be prepared to anticipate as many questions as possible. It is always better to consider your responses ahead of time.
- Will there be media present? If so, will your agency allow you to speak with them?

Retirements

– As a guest speaker, master of ceremonies, or award presenter:

- Which role are you playing?
- How many retirees will be represented? Whether this is a single retirement ceremony or multiple personnel retirements, obtain as much biographical information on each retiree.

- Do you know the retiree you are celebrating? If you don't, then find out as much as you can. The retirement ceremony is an important day for the retiree and their family, and you don't want to trivialize it by demonstrating you don't know the person. Unfortunately, when a retiree finally gets to that time in their life, many of those coworkers and managers who best know them are not there at the end of a person's career. That is unfortunate, and that is why it is essential for those who will speak at the podium to be prepared to make it a memorable experience for the retiree(s).
- Is there any significant event in the retiree's career that is worth noting? This information may be available in the retiree's personnel file. Celebrate any of those significant events. Most of the audience probably will not be aware of them.
- Are there person's in the audience who would like to say a few words? Plan this ahead of time in the interest of time. Otherwise, it is embarrassing if a request for anyone to come up and share some words on the retiree's behalf, and no one volunteers, or too many want to talk and causes the event to drag on.

Eulogies

A eulogy is the most emotional and honorable speech you can give. The focus is both on the deceased and the family and friends the deceased left behind. Recognizing that in the criminal justice profession we are called upon far too many times to celebrate our brothers and sisters who lose their lives protecting those they serve, I thought it necessary to add eulogies as a type of speech we are called upon in the performance of our duties. Having myself delivered nine eulogies in recent years, I created a short questionnaire form I use when interviewing the family and friends of the deceased to help me prepare the eulogy. That may sound a little cold, but as stated earlier, organization and preparation are essential to delivering a successful, well-received speech. Here are the questions I ask on the form:

Full name of the deceased: _____
- Date of Birth: Place of Birth:
- Schools attended:
    - Elementary –
    - Middle/Jr. High School –
    - High School –
    - Colleges –
    - Training

- Different jobs they had:
- Organization memberships:
- Hobbies or outside interests:
- What would you like the people at the memorial service to know about your loved one? For example, impressive achievements in their life, something special they may have done for you, or what they meant to you.
- Is there a funny story about the deceased, or a funny story they may have told you that you remember?
- What particular words, sayings, nicknames, or phrases did they use that you may remember?
- Are there any particular dates or events in their life that you feel should be mentioned?
- Are there any specific work-related events that should be mentioned?
- Is there a short poem, saying, or quote that you might have that is appropriate for this occasion?

Eulogies are very emotional to deliver because it is a speech given by someone close to the subject. It is not uncommon to be emotional and tear up while speaking. Some get so overwhelmed that they can't continue. If you feel tears coming on, there is a trick you can use to stop your tears. First, stop talking and press the emotional reset button — with your tongue. "Simply push your tongue to the roof of your mouth, and you will instantly stop crying," says Janine Driver, chief executive of the Body Language Institute in Washington, D.C.[3] I read about this the night I was writing my mother's eulogy. I was concerned that my emotions would get the best of me and I didn't want that to happen. I tried the tongue pressed against the roof of my mouth, and it worked for me. It really worked. I recently shared this trick with a family member, and he told me it worked for him also while delivering a father's toast at his daughter's wedding. So try it if you must. You have nothing to lose.

PERSUASIVE

A persuasive speech usually comes your way as a result of some requirement that falls within your purview. There are three types of persuasive speeches that are used to convince an audience of something presented by the speaker: a factual persuasive speech, a value persuasive speech, and a policy persuasive speech. Indeed, in the criminal justice field we see all three. For example, attorneys in a criminal case presenting their arguments to persuade a jury use the factual persuasive speech; a value speech example is when the US Congress political opposition parties were trying to persuade the American people that President Donald J. Trump was or was not involved in activities that were considered impeachable actions. A valuable persuasive speech can be about whether something is right or wrong. It may question the moral or ethical aspect of an issue, and a policy persuasion speech example would be the goal of convincing a group to agree with your interpretation of a policy. In all three types you are mostly trying to sway the audience to adopt your viewpoint.

You recall that a speech is made up of three distinct parts: intro-duction, body, and summary. A persuasive speech has three sub-headings within each of these parts. They are *problem, solution,* and *benefit.* These three points create the foundation for develop-ing your persuasive speech. The questions that need to be asked by the speaker while developing the address are:
- Who is your audience? Who are the decision-makers?
- What do you want the audience to do as a result of the speech?
- What is the problem for which your information is the solution?
- What is a brief story, anecdote, statistic, factoid, or question that sums up the problem?

The following is an example of when I codelivered a persuasive speech with another speaker. At the time, I was the director of the Office of Occupational Health, Environmental and Safety Services (OHESS) for a federal agency that was made up entirely of secure spaces requiring security clearance for access. For an ambulance to respond to an office space for a medical emergency, the police department had to be notified to meet the ambulance at the fence and escort the ambulance to where the employee needed emer-gency care. There was a time when we had several employees die of cardiac arrest within a short period of time. There was con-cern that there was time being wasted for the ambulance getting through the control points to get to the subject needing emergency care. This was the same time when new defibrillator technology was being introduced; an automated external defibrillator (AED) that could be used by nonmedical staff. We researched the AED and believed it was our answer to better respond to medical emer-gencies inside our secure facilities. The only problem was getting

160

the money to procure enough AEDs to service all the agency's locations. It was near the end of the government fiscal year, and there were no extra funds to be had. That didn't stop us from trying. We were talking about people's lives here. So I contacted my technical director, a cardiologist, and we prepared a persuasive speech to be given to the Leadership Council, which had the authority to find and give us the funds we needed.

The following was the data we used to develop content for our persuasive speech given to the Leadership Council:

Problem
- Employees were dying of cardiac arrest in the workplace.
- Time was wasted responding to the victims.
- Statistics showed that cardiopulmonary resuscitation (CPR) is only useful 5 to 7 minutes after the onset of cardiac arrest.
- Data showed that it was taking 8 to 12 minutes to get to the location of the medical emergency.

Solution
- Train responding police officers to use the automated external defibrillator (AED).
- Police officers can reduce response time to the victim.
- Response time would be reduced from 8 to 12 minutes to 1 to 4 minutes.
- OHESS had the authority, training, and skills to be able to be the first in the state to train nonmedical professionals (in this case, police officers) to use this new medical technology.

Benefit
- Using the AED would demonstrate an ability to respond to medical emergencies in a more efficient and timely manner.
- We determined that statistically, the average age of our audience, the Leadership Council, was in the middle of the age group that was more likely to suffer from cardiac arrest, therefore more likely to benefit from the procurement of AEDs.
- While presenting the speech, without anyone in the room being made aware of what was about to happen, several police officers burst into the room with two-way radios blaring, carrying an AED with them. They were simulating a response to a cardiac arrest patient. While the audience had their attention toward the door and the officers entering the room, I placed an AED training dummy in the middle of the conference table that

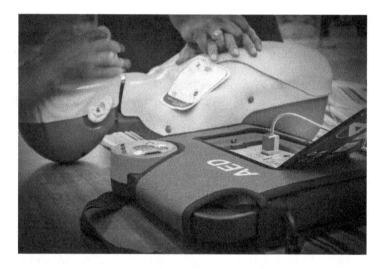

Figure 8.8 Demonstrating the use of an automated external defibrillator (AED). (From Shutterstock.)

was being hidden from their sight under the table. The officers quickly moved several of the council members from the table and began attaching the AED to the dummy and began administering first aid with the use of the AED. See Figure 8.8.

- The demonstration grabbed the audience's attention and allowed them to see firsthand how the AED worked.

Summary

- The audience was impressed with the demonstration.
- They believed the data presented. Remember, my cospeaker was a cardiologist. They believed everything he said. Being believable is most important in a persuasive speech.
- One week from the close of the fiscal year, with no funds available, we received all the money we needed to fund the project.
- No one in the room was willing to say no to this project. Why? Because we made it personal. AEDs could save lives, their lives.

TESTIMONIAL

Expert Testimony

The word *testimony* is from the Latin root word *testis*, meaning "witness." Expert testimony is the oral response made by a qualified person about a scientific, technical, or professional issue. It's more of an answer to a question than a speech. The speaker controls a speech; expert testimony is controlled by the person asking the question. It is never read, unless it is congressional testimony, discussed later. The following are actions that should be used when giving testimony:

- Refresh your memory during preparation. Remember, if you are going to be using notes while up on the witness stand, those notes will be shared with the opposing counsel.
- Speak in your own words, but do not use words that are so technical that they will not be understood by the trier of fact (judge and/or jury). Do not use acronyms unless you state them first.

On December 2, 1991, William Kennedy Smith's rape trial began. Smith, a nephew of President John F. Kennedy, then a 30-year-old medical student at Georgetown University, was accused of sexually assaulting a 29-year-old Florida woman in the early hours of March 30, 1991, at the Kennedy family's Palm Beach compound.

During the trial, which was one of the first to be televised live, the victim's identity was electronically obscured with a large white dot to protect her privacy. She gave very detailed testimony of the event and was considered an excellent witness on the stand. But unfortunately, because DNA was relatively new and DNA evidence was collected and examined, the prosecution called upon the expert witness who tested the DNA to testify to the whole process. Lengthy laborious technical testimony was given that appeared to bore the jury and everyone else in the courtroom. Smith had never denied having consensual sex with the victim, so what was the DNA evidence going to prove. I am mentioning this here because too much time had passed between the excellent testimony from the victim and the lengthy technical testimony from the expert. That may have hurt the prosecution case in hindsight. Smith was acquitted of all charges.

- Speak clearly so that you can be heard and understood.
- Do not exaggerate.
- Listen carefully to each question asked and only answer the question asked.
- If you don't understand what is being asked, have them repeat the question.
- If you don't know the answer, admit it right away.

- If you are not qualified as an expert, you only can testify to facts. Only qualified experts can give an opinion.
- Respond orally to the questions. Don't nod your head or use filler words to give answers; the court recorder in the courtroom will not pick that up.
- Think before you speak. Don't be afraid to pause before you respond to formulate your response.
- Do not volunteer information. That can get you into trouble. Just answer the question asked of you.
- Be positive and confident.
- Be polite to the person asking the questions even if they are discourteous towards you.
- Have good eye contact with the person asking the question.

On one occasion, I was testifying in federal court in an evidence suppression hearing as a consultant for the defense. They were trying to get specific photo-array evidence disqualified for trial. The defense attorney instructed me to direct my responses to the judge. He wanted me to have eye contact with the judge at all times. His justification for this was that the judge was the one who would be making the ruling on the evidence, so he wanted me to direct my testimony to the judge. So in the middle of my testimony, while being questioned by the prosecutor, the judge stopped me and asked why I was looking at him rather than looking at the prosecutor who was asking me the questions. I just said, "Sorry, your honor," and turned my chair toward the front where the prosecutor was standing. In doing so, one of the four legs of the chair moved off the platform where I was sitting, and I fell backward almost falling off the platform on to the floor. I grabbed on to the witness stand railing and saved myself. I learned two things that day. Always have eye contact with the person asking you a question, and don't move the witness chair from where it is positioned.

Congressional Testimony

Review the following 12 tips for testifying before the United States Congress, provided with permission by Dr. Charles Blahous, the J. Fish and Lillian F. Smith Chair and Senior Research Strategist at the Mercatus

Center, a visiting fellow with the Hoover Institution, and a contributor to E21.

THE DIRTY DOZEN: 12 TIPS FOR TESTIFYING BEFORE CONGRESS[4]

- *#1: Be selective; only testify if you have genuine expertise to offer.* Testifying before Congress is a rarely granted honor and difficult to pass up. Nevertheless, it is better to decline an invitation than to waste committee members' time, or still worse, to embarrass yourself by being unable to satisfy their desire for useful information. Be honest with committee staff and with yourself about whether you have genuine expertise on any subject about which you might be questioned in a hearing format.

- *#2: Written testimony is not a forum for conducting original research.* The written statement you submit should consist only of material you verified long before the hearing. If you are researching an aspect of the subject for the first time when drafting your testimony, this means you do not already have the requisite expertise in it. By all means, include original and compelling passages in your written testimony. But the substantive material contained within it should be only that which you had already mastered and substantiated before you accepted the invitation.

- *#3: Draft a separate oral version of your testimony.* The typical procedure is that you will submit a written statement before testifying and then at the hearing deliver a time-limited opening statement usually lasting no more than five minutes. Your oral statement should draw from the material in your written testimony but it should be a separately written document. Practice delivering it, practice it again, and then practice it some more, timing yourself on each run. If you're like me, a statement written to be five minutes long will last closer to 7–8 minutes the first few times you rehearse. Practice and prune as necessary until you can consistently deliver it in five minutes (ideally in four and a half) without rushing. By the time you appear, you should be reciting your statement in a conversational tone more than you are reading it, so that you can effectively engage your audience during delivery.

- *#4: Pick three main points to emphasize in your oral statement.* Do not attempt to cover all of your written testimony's content in your verbal remarks. Decide on the three or so primary things you think are most important for committee members to know, and focus on those. You needn't give exactly 100 seconds to each of your three points, but try to come reasonably close. If you give

165

too much or too little time to any single point, your cogency will suffer. I typically write down, at three or four places in the printed version of my oral remarks, the amount of time I want to have elapsed by the time I reach each point, to keep track of whether I am proceeding at the desired pace.

- *#5: This is not about you, and especially not about your opinions.* Your job in testifying is to provide information; it is not to explain why members of Congress should have the same opinions about an issue that you do. Remember the old adage about opinions. They're like belly buttons: everybody's got one. You're there because you have expertise to offer, not because your opinions are better than anybody else's. The only time you should offer a subjective opinion is if you are directly asked to do so. Otherwise, focus on providing information that can inform the legislative process.

- *#6: Prepare answers to questions you are likely to receive.* Talk to staff ahead of time, ideally on both sides of the aisle, about questions their members have an interest in asking you. Ask your own colleagues if they are willing to send you examples of questions to be ready for. You don't necessarily need to write out detailed answers to them all, but you should know how you intend to answer each one. Obviously, it's impossible to antici-pate every possible question you might be asked. Nevertheless, it's almost certain you will spend more time preparing for the hearing than any one member does. It's actually quite possible for you to get through an entire hearing without receiving a single question you hadn't prepared for.

- *#7: Be respectful of the committee members' time.* A member's time in a hearing is an extremely precious commodity. You might be sitting at the witness table for hours, but a specific member might be given only five minutes to question you. That's likely the only time the member's constituents and hometown press will see them performing at the hearing. Respect every second of that time. Keep your answers short. Watch the member while you're speaking, and be ready to clam up if they are itching to jump in. If the member wants to spend the entire time talking rather than questioning you, don't get in their way.

- *#8: Prioritize information useful to committee members on both sides of the aisle.* It's typical for witnesses to be invited by one side or the other, meaning by the majority or the minority party. But regardless of which side invited you, your job is to provide information to the entire committee. You are likely doing your job well if you provide information that committee members on both sides of the aisle use to make opposing policy arguments.

This means your information is deemed credible and is providing a factual foundation for the policy debate.

- *#9: Don't bluff.* Remember that your primary obligation at all times is to be truthful. You can't offer truth where you don't know it. If a committee member asks you a question that you don't know the answer to, admit it, and offer to follow up after the hearing. Do not guess, unless specifically asked to do so, and unless you make clear to everyone that you're guessing.

- *#10: Don't interject when committee members are not looking for you to do so.* There will likely be many times during a hearing when a member or another witness says something you believe glosses over a key aspect of an issue. By all means, fill in an information gap if a question has been thrown open to all the witnesses at the table, but otherwise, restrain yourself unless asked directly. If a member presents a one-sided view of an issue, it's the job of members across the aisle, not yours, to present the other side. It's totally appropriate to say privately to staff before or even during a hearing that there are certain things you would like to be asked. But when in front of the microphone, only pipe up if you are asked (or in the very rare instance that your silence would signal tacit agreement with a mischaracterization of your statements). It's a better outcome for a point to be left unexplored than for a member to misperceive you as playing a partisan role.

- *#11: Printed material is good to have on hand for study purposes, but is rarely used during the hearing itself.* I tend to load up on printed reference material, to feel secure and fully informed while at the witness table. However, its principal utility comes during the process of compiling and studying it prior to the hearing. It's almost never the case that you will have time during questioning to rifle through a tall stack of papers searching for a substantive detail. Anything you don't know off the top of your head is best dealt with in follow-up exchanges.

- *#12: Visit the restroom right before the hearing begins, and go easy on the coffee.* Congressional hearings can sometimes last for several hours without a break.

Impromptu and Extemporaneous

When these two terms are associated with public speaking, they have different meanings. An impromptu speech is when the speaker is called upon to say a few words without having made any preparation. Extemporaneous speech means delivering a prepared speech without notes. They are two very different methods for speaking that are generally believed to be the same. So now that we have made the distinction, let us discuss each one.

Impromptu

Impromptu speaking is more of a situation you may find yourself in rather than as a method of delivery. Depending upon your experience, occupation, interests, and authority, you should have some awareness of the possibility that you could be called upon "to say a few words," or it's just your desire to say something at a meeting or event. Although we think of the impromptu speech as something that was thrust upon us with no prior notice, are they really? If you are going to a town hall meeting representing your department and have no formal requirement to speak, would it be unusual to have someone ask you a question or ask your opinion on some issue that is associated with the theme and intent of the town hall meeting? I think not. What about a meeting? Your required presence at the meeting is enough to expect a reason to be asked to speak. If you are a manager, there are numerous times when you are asked to share your opinion on an issue or celebrate someone's birthday, promotion, award, or a holiday event. Attending memorial services are a time when you can be asked or volunteer to say something about the dearly departed. Wedding toasts can be either impromptu or extemporaneous depending on your role. I must say, there are far too many toasts being given at weddings these days, so you always need to be prepared.

So how do you prepare for the impromptu speech? Mark Twain, American humorist and author, once said, "It takes me at least three weeks to prepare an impromptu speech."[5] A friend of Winston Churchill's, R. E. Smith, said, "Winston has spent the best years of his life writing impromptu speeches."[6] Always anticipate the possibility before you are at the venue. Visualize yourself being asked to say something and think about what you would say. Never begin by apologizing for not being prepared. Remember, you are not expected to be prepared, it's an impromptu utterance you are delivering, not the Gettysburg Address. Be aware of the latest thinking on an issue. Focus your thoughts on the subject and the occasion. Comment on topical views by others in attendance. Toastmasters International, a worldwide organization promoting communication, and public speaking and leadership skills, has included in their general membership meeting what it refers to as "Table Topics." Several Table Topics will be presented at a meeting unknown by the membership except for the one member who was assigned to make them up for that particular meeting. The Table

Topicsmaster will select a member to stand, and they will be given a short Table Topic that is only one to five words in length. They, in turn, have one to three minutes to talk about it. It provides excellent practice to develop impromptu skills. Toastmasters lists in its "Speak Off the Cuff" module to consider patterns of ideas in your mind and associate them with the topic.

Those pattern ideas are:[7]

- Compare past and present with a possible conjecture about the future.
- Contrast a before and after situation.
- You might approach the topic from alternative viewpoints of life's stages: childhood, adolescence, adulthood, old age.
- State the problem and suggest a solution.
- Compare the advantages and disadvantages.
- Consider the political, economic, or social aspects of the topic.
- Consider geographical influences – city, state, country, world.

I was a member of Toastmasters in the 1980s and competed in several speech contests. On one particular occasion, November 13, 1982, to be exact, I competed in a District Level "Table Topics" competition and won first prize. There were four contestants, who were removed from the banquet room, then called in one at a time, so we didn't know what the table topic was until you were standing in front of the large crowd. We all received the same topic. Now, remember, the table topic can only be a phrase one to five words in length. The topic for the competition was the word "Nothing." Yes, the word "nothing" was the topic. I had to speak three full minutes on the word "nothing." My first thought was just to stand there and say nothing for 3 minutes, but I was afraid one of the other contestants might have thought of that already. So I stood tall before the crowd and began my dissertation on "nothing." I don't remember a word of what I said, but it must have been more entertaining somehow then the others. After that evening, I never was concerned with impromptu speaking. Open your mouth, and just let the words flow out!

Extemporaneous

Extemporaneous speaking is when you have mastered your speech, probably delivered it many times over, and don't need any notes to deliver it. Of course, if you are using slides, the slides actually become your notes, but

Figure 8.9 District 18, Table Topics Contest, 1st Place Winner Trophy. (Photo by Luiz Santos.)

you still are comfortable and smooth in your delivery. For example, I have been teaching a general survey course in forensic sciences for 42 years. Nothing has changed that much that I can't open my mouth and speak without stopping. It's not that I have memorized the content, I now live and breathe it. I guess that comes with age and experience, but remember, good speakers are made not born.

CHAPTER REVIEW REFLECTION TOOLS

1. In an informational speech, know what you want the audience to do with the information you deliver.
2. Breakfast, luncheon, and dinner speeches are the most difficult to deliver because of the inherent distractions going on in the room.

3. Plenary sessions, also referred to as general sessions, are presentations given at a conference in which all members attending the conference are invited.
4. A scientific research poster is sometimes referred to as a conference poster because that is where they are usually presented.
5. The three most essential prerequisites for visual images placed on scientific posters are that they be carefully prepared, simple, and necessary in the storyline.
6. Scientists and technical people tend to be left-brained thinkers, meaning they are very analytical and methodical in their communication.
7. A persuasive speech has three subheadings within each of these parts. They are problem, solution, and benefit.
8. Expert testimony is controlled by the person asking the questions to the expert.
9. An impromptu speech is when the speaker is called upon to say a few words without having made any preparation.
10. An extemporaneous speech means delivering a prepared speech without notes.

NOTES

1. The topic on the show had to do with the Brandon Mayfield case. Brandon Mayfield was the Nebraska attorney whose fingerprint was incorrectly identified by three Federal Bureau of Investigation fingerprint experts as being positively identified with a latent fingerprint found on a detonator bag associated with the terrorist train bombings in 2004 in Madrid, Spain. They were wrong. Brandon Mayfield, who was a Muslim convert, was held in jail for over two weeks because of their mistake. The news reporter was trying to make the point that because of this mistake, all fingerprint evidence should no longer be used in a court of law. She asked me several different ways to agree that fingerprints should not be used in a court of law because of this mistake. I didn't agree, so they found an attorney in Baltimore who would agree with her, to a point that when she asked the attorney, "If the Spanish police had not actually found the real person who left that fingerprint, where would Braydon Mayfield be today?" The attorney stated on the show, "There is no question that Mr. Mayfield would be sentenced to either to life, or sentenced to death, no question." Its statements like that one that makes television news so entertaining, not accurate, but certainly entertaining.

2. Robert R. H. Anholt, *Dazzle 'Em with Style: The Art of Oral Scientific Presentation*, 2nd ed., Elsevier Academic Press, 2006. Bullets taken from "Important Points to Remember," pp. 115–117.
3. For more information on this topic, see Janek Tuttar, "How to Give a Speech Without Crying?: 10 Great Tips", https://speakandconquer.com/how-to-give-a-speech-without-crying/.
4. Charles Blahous, "The Dirty Dozen: 12 Tips for Testifying Before Congress," Commentary, E21 Manhattan Institute, June 25, 2019, https://economics21.org/12-tips-for-testifying-before-congress.
5. Lilly Walters, *Secrets of Successful Speakers*, January 1995, p. 32.
6. William Manchester, *The Last Lion: Winston Spencer Churchill*, Dell, 1983, p. 32.
7. Toastmasters International, Inc., Specialty Speeches, Advanced Communication and Leadership Program, Module 1, 1979, p. 5.

9

Preparing for News Media Interviews and Entertainment Documentaries

INTRODUCTION

Chapter 9 discusses how the criminal justice professional should prepare and deliver information when interviewed by the media. The role of the police department public information officer (PIO) is also discussed. The chapter also provides direction when asked to do an on-camera scripted or unscripted TV documentary (Figure 9.1).

No criminal justice professional can begin a discussion on how to work with the media without first mentioning the "CSI effect"[1] and what it has done to help and hinder the profession.

> Crime and courtroom proceedings have long been fodder for film and television scriptwriters. In recent years, however, the media's use of the courtroom as a vehicle for drama has not only proliferated; it has changed focus. In apparent fascination with our criminal justice process, many of today's courtroom dramas are *based on* actual cases.[2]

The key phrase is "based on," meaning it has elements of reality but not factual. Here lies the issue. Both the criminal justice professional and the general public need to understand that Hollywood and the entire broadcasting industry is in the business to "entertain" their consumers, not "educate" them. When they are producing a show, if the facts get in the way of entertainment, entertainment always wins. I have experienced that

Figure 9.1   Multi facets of news outlets. (From Shutterstock.)

numerous times as an on-camera consultant. When I am asked to comment on a local or national news event, there never seems to be a specific reason for me being there. While the cameraman is setting up the equipment, the news commentator will ask me, "So, what should I be asking you?" My response on every occasion is, "I don't know. You asked me here to do this interview." In spite of the lack of reporting of real information, we still need to be as prepared as best as possible.

TELEVISION AND RADIO NEWS INTERVIEWS

When the call comes to you to be interviewed for some current event, find out what the event is and research as much information as you can find about it. The interview questions that will be asked are generally open-ended questions that become short speeches. That is why we are discussing them here in this book. Sometimes the voice on the phone who asked you to do the interview (a producer) will be able to give you some specifics on what you will be asked, but the person who does the interview may not have the same interest. Don't be surprised by this; prepare yourself as best as possible. If you are being recorded for later broadcast, you can be assured that your comments will be edited. For example, a 10-minute recorded interview will yield about 10 seconds of airtime on average. Don't have your feelings hurt by this; it's normal (Figure 9.2).

When you are doing a live interview, you are on your own. There will be no one to help you with cue cards. So be prepared with as much

Figure 9.2 Depicted here is author, Tom Mauriello, being interviewed by news anchor Vic Carter, WJZ-TV, Baltimore, Maryland. (Courtesy of WJZ-TV, CBS Corporation.)

background information as possible. I did a local news broadcast on one occasion where they asked me to come to the studio to do the interview live. I got there in plenty of time because I assumed that someone was going to give me some background on the case they wanted me to discuss. It was five minutes to airtime, and I was finally introduced to the person that was going to interview me live. I asked him if he could give me a hint on what he was going to ask me, and he said, "I wish I could, but I don't know yet." Needless to say, the one-minute interview was a complete impromptu discussion.

Remember, as stated earlier, most of the time you are being interviewed, it is being recorded, and the interview will be edited at a later time, so don't worry about any mistakes you may have made. During the interview, when asked a question, if you are not sure how to answer, stop talking, think about if for a moment, and then speak. The pause will be edited out, so don't worry about that small stuff.

If the media asks you a question that is inappropriate and may expose investigative information that should remain protected, advise the interviewer that you are unable to respond to that question because it is currently under investigation. I get asked to be interviewed all the time because of my university affiliation. I find that television and radio news interviews are time fillers where they are looking for a talking head or voice with some sort of expertise to say something that may be controversial or provocative. I like to think it is to be informative also, but I question that sometimes. Many times when a criminal act is ongoing, the media will look for anyone to say anything on the air. Be careful not to provide any information that would be detrimental to the identification and apprehension of a criminal(s). Don't expose any information directly or indirectly that will hamper an investigation.

Many times the story the media is working on has a specific hypothesis they are trying to satisfy, and they are interviewing you to try to get you to make statements that support their hypothesis and conclusions. Don't be bullied into saying something that you don't believe. Answer their questions the best you can, and if they try to get you do answer something a different way, tell them you have responded to their question.

When you have a clear interest in getting specific information across during the interview, take the initiative, and consider the following:

- Set a clear goal for every interview. Don't assume the reporter will ask you questions that will have you explaining your points of view.
- Take the initiative during the interview to get your point across. Many times at the end of an interview, the reporter will ask if there is anything else that needs to be discussed. Take that opportunity to do just that. It may not make the final cut, but at least you tried.
- Keep your answers short and memorable. You select the best response to the reporter's question in a manner that supports what you believe is best for the listeners. Remember, you are the subject matter expert, not the reporter.
- Speak about what you know. The reporter will, many times, ask for your opinion on something ongoing. Be careful not to speculate on something you have no knowledge of or authority to speak on that is happening in the present. The media is always looking for any information or speculation about an ongoing incident about what the police may be doing or what the perpetrator is doing. Don't comment on something you don't know.

PUBLIC INFORMATION OFFICER (PIO) REPORTING

Over the past 30 years, the nature of the news media business has changed dramatically. The development of 24-hour cable news coverage, camera phones, and, of course, social media has added to the ever-expanding field of information contributing to news reporting. This has created new challenges for the public information officer (PIO) in all criminal justice fields. Today, PIOs have expanded responsibilities, which include providing timely, on-the-scene reporting that requires impromptu reporting of criminal activities, many times as they are happening.[3] You don't have to be the PIO of your department to be called upon to speak to reporters, so one should always be prepared.

- Communication skills for a PIO[4]
    - Keep it simple and short (referred to as the KISS principle) using easily understood terms
    - Express empathy and care[5]
    - Balance negative information with at least three positive pieces of information[6]
    - Be sensitive and responsive to the perceptions and concerns of the stakeholders

Captain Paul R. Starks, retired from the Montgomery County Maryland Police Department after over 34 years of service, spent his last 11 years assigned to the Public Information Office, retiring as its director. The Montgomery County Police Department has over 1,300 officers serving a large suburban county to the west of Washington, D.C. (Figure 9.3). Captain Starks is not only a colleague, but he is also a former student of mine, a graduate of the University of Maryland Department of Criminology and Criminal Justice.

Figure 9.3 Capt. Paul R, Starks, Montgomery County Maryland Police Department, Director of Public Information Office. (Photograph courtesy of Montgomery Community Media.)

I spent a morning interviewing Captain Starks for this chapter of the book to tap into his knowledge and experience to understand what skills and abilities are needed to develop into a successful PIO. I wanted to know what worked for him and how did he recognize success. I assumed that most PIO presentations were read verbatim or impromptu because of the nature of PIO activities. His response was quite different than what I expected. He said he always tried not to read at a PIO conference, but instead to tell the incident like a story to the media. At that point, I let him know that Aristotle would be proud to hear that from him, and so was I. He stated that it was easier for him to remember the key points that needed to be made when he prepared and presented the incident in a story format. He also reiterated the communications skills mentioned earlier as necessary: to keep the PIO report simple, express empathy and care, balance the adverse event being reported with three positive actions that were being taken, and be sensitive to the concerns of all the stakeholders.

The most significant experience Captain Starks had to share was the need to communicate with and create good relationships with the media. He said it is always better to be ahead of any request for information from the media, so that way you are in a position to "tell your own story," rather than having the media deciding that for you.[7]

ON-CAMERA SCRIPTED AND UNSCRIPTED DIALOGUE

When asked to participate in a television documentary, an on-camera *scripted* dialogue means that you will be given specific lines to read on a teleprompter or with cue cards. Make sure that you review the text completely before the shoot because those words will become your words on the show. If you don't agree with portions of the text, discuss it with the producer or director of the show. Do not say anything on camera that you feel is not correct or reasonable. Don't rely on the production company to protect you in this regard. The company's objective to entertain is more important to them, than your need to be factually correct (Figure 9.4).

Unscripted dialogue is when you respond to a program director's question or when you are asked to comment on some issue while the camera is rolling. It is entirely impromptu. If you say something that is not correct or you believe it is inaccurate, then tell them right away. It can easily be edited out. You are not expected to be a trained actor, so do your best to be relaxed, have a good time, and present yourself well.

FILM MAKING

Figure 9.4   Film cameraman. (From Shutterstock.)

Video production companies don't always have makeup staff available on the set, so do your best to make sure your hair is in place and your clothing neat and clean. Don't wear bright colors or loud prints. No white dress shirts or blouses. Ask the production company if it has any specific instructions for you about your appearance.

You do not get an opportunity to view the recorded show before it is aired. TV shows are not recorded in any particular sequence, so you never really know how the show will be presented until you view it on the day of the premiere airing of the show.

CHAPTER REVIEW REFLECTION TOOLS

1. When you are doing a live interview with the media, you are on your own.
2. A 10-minute recorded interview will yield about 10 seconds of airtime on average.
3. Most of the time you are being interviewed, it is being recorded, and the interview will be edited at a later time, so don't worry about any slipups you may have made.
4. An on-camera scripted dialogue means that you will be given specific lines to read on a teleprompter or with cue cards.

5. Unscripted dialogue is when you respond to a program director's questions or when you are asked to comment on some issue while the camera is rolling. It is entirely impromptu.

NOTES

1. The CSI effect theory asserts that popular TV crime dramas that focus on forensic science may affect the behavior and expectations of jurors in real-life cases. The theory also suggests that jurors' perceptions of the need for specific forensic evidence may impact their decisions in the courtroom. National Forensic Science Technology Center, "CSI Effect Theory: New Website," www.nfstc.org/csi-effect-theory-new-website/.
2. Honorable Donald Shelton, "The 'CSI Effect': Does It Really Exist?" National Institute of Justice, March 16, 2008.
3. See Chapter 8 for detailed information for delivering impromptu presentations.
4. These skills have been validated in several hundred behavioral and neuroscience research studies as stated by Dr. Vincent Covello in his video series, "Communication Skills for Pubic Information Officers (PIOs) in Risk and Crisis Situations," Drexel University, Dornsife School of Public Health, Center for Public Health Readiness and Communication, www.youtube.com/watch?v=VcjsF5P4fbA.
5. Theodore Roosevelt's phrase "nobody cares how much you know, until they know how much you care," suggests here that no one wants to listen to what you have to say unless they can see what you're willing to do.
6. This is based on the 1N = 3P Template, created by Professor Daniel Kahneman, a psychologist and economist notable for his work on the psychology of judgment and decision-making as well as behavioral economics, for which he was awarded the 2002 Nobel Memorial Prize in Economic Sciences. In order to balance a negative you have to introduce at least three positive pieces of information. It is referred to as the "loss aversion theory." It takes three positives to offset one negative. So if you, as a PIO, have one bad piece of information to report, you should include three or four pieces of good information to balance the negative.
7. Captain Paul Starks's quote here means that when you are regularly communicating with the media, you won't get blindsided by a question or comment you were not expecting. Therefore, you can prepare your presentation and tell your story the way you see best.

10

Teaching Academic and Training Courses

INTRODUCTION

Chapter 10 focuses on methods of teaching criminal justice and forensic sciences classes as an academic course referred to as the *pedagogy* of teaching, and also methods of teaching criminal justice and forensic sciences focused on the development of skills training. This chapter is not only for the criminal justice professional teaching in the field of their expertise but also for those high school and college science and social studies teachers who find themselves assigned to teach criminal justice and forensic sciences type courses. In most cases they have no experience or background in these fields. The difference between education and training is defined and how one can overlap the other determined by the objectives of the tasker. The author's 45-plus years of teaching academic courses and law enforcement and counterintelligence training courses provide examples and proven techniques that have evolved over the years. From the standup traditional platform lecture method to the blended and online learning methods, all are discussed in this chapter for the reader's consideration. Course and syllabus development, lecture content development, text and workbook selection, sample laboratory exercises, and inviting guest lecturers into the classroom are the topics discussed in this all-encompassing chapter.

Let's first distinguish the difference between education and training. The best example I can use to clarify the difference in your mind is to ask you the question, "Would you rather your child receive sex educa-tion or sex training in their school?" Although you may not want either, I think you get the point. Education, received in an academic institution, is all about learning strategies and theatrical principles in a career field or activity, whereas training focuses on practice and learning those skills necessary to accomplish a specific job. Education teaches you the history of the who, what, where, when, and, most important, why a subject is essential for the student to learn, and training teaches you the rules and practices used to complete a technical task. The end result for an educa-tional student is they learn a subject in a strategic global manner, and the training student learns a subject in a hands-on tactical manner necessary to complete a task.

The social sciences, such as criminology and criminal justice aca-demic courses, all too often only focus on teaching theory. Still, the bio-logical and physical sciences and technology courses teach both theory and practice. The social science career fields leave the training to be done by employers after a student graduates and is hired. Training is done in police academies, internships, and professional certification programs.

So when preparing to teach an academic course or deliver a lecture, consider whether you are asked to educate or train your audience. Today's learning and teaching technologies offer a wide range of methods that can be used. As you read through this chapter, remember that today's stu-dents have learned to learn differently than many of us who are educators and trainers. I have had the opportunity to have been teaching and speak-ing to students and professional groups for over 45 years. I have seen it all, experienced it all, and learned to adjust. Don't ever forget: It's not about you; it's about your customers, the students, and audiences that you touch with your knowledge, skills, and abilities.

THE TRADITIONAL LECTURE

What was most satisfying about teaching for me over the years was lectur-ing to large lecture halls full of impressionable students, who were eager to learn by the spoken word. For many of the 45-plus years I had been teaching college, lecturing was the standard method for delivering course content. It was a blend of lecturing and textbook readings. In the '80s, we used lecture notes sitting in front of us on the lectern and wrote on the chalkboard to list important facts. Some of the more creative instructors would use transparencies projected on a screen with an overhead projector. We would lug a 16mm film projector to show training films when appropriate. In the '90s, we were able to create detailed 35mm slides that projected on a screen and were able to eliminate the need for lecture notes because the slides took the place of our written notes. We stopped using 16mm films and replaced them with videotapes played on video cassette recorders (VCRs) that were installed in all the lecture halls. Then finally, with the advent of computers, video projectors, and PowerPoint software, we transformed all our instructional media onto PowerPoint presentations, hyperlinking video shows and online clips into one slide show program. The technology was changing during these years and that required teachers to do the same. More important, the students were changing. What was changing about them was the way they wanted to learn. They no longer want to be talked to during a predetermined time of the day and week. They wanted to get their content on their terms. Laptops and mobile devices are now able to provide them with all the electronic content that a lecturer could present in the lecture hall. They are looking for more interactive learning opportunities.

I noticed this change in my student's learning habits around the year 2005. I used to pride myself in being able to engage students, and have them ask questions and comments on content being presented both live in the lecture hall and in their textbook readings. Then this began to stop. There were no more questions, no comments, and students were now paying more attention to their laptops and mobile devices that had email, text messages, and internet sites on them that had nothing to do with the course. Some questions did come later in the evening when I went home. I would get emails or texts from students asking questions about the information I had lectured about earlier that evening in the lecture hall. Two-way communication just stopped in the lecture hall. I was doing all the talking and I didn't know if they were even listening.

The standard lecture still exists today, so for those of you who are still more comfortable with it, go ahead if you must. I assure you your students are missing out on your ability to share your knowledge and expertise in so many new and exciting ways. I love speaking to large groups of people in large rooms, and this still happens for me when I am a guest speaker in a classroom or lecture hall. But don't forget, today's classrooms and lecture halls are slowly being transformed into spaces that look quite different then we have been used to, as discussed in Part I, Chapters 4, 5, and 6.

THE BLENDED (HYBRID) LEARNING FORMAT

The *blended learning method* for teaching is a means to move away from the live lecture format to a technique that uses technology to deliver content in a manner that satisfies today's students. Blended (hybrid) learning is a formal education program in which a student learns at least in part through online delivery of content and instruction with some element of student control over time, place, and pace. I first learned of blended learning when I was experiencing students less engaged in the live lecture, and I was the only one talking. I was looking for an answer to solve this issue, and that is when I was introduced to the blended learning format (Figure 10.1).

The course I teach is Introduction to Criminalistics. I decided that I would record all my lectures, have the students view them each week at their pleasure, and then spend 100% of class time conducting interactive, hands-on practical exercises.

The first step for a blended course is to obtain a video editing software. The software will allow you to do four things simultaneously: It records your PowerPoint slides, records your voice while lecturing, records you while talking, and finally records any video clips used previously in the lecture hall. I had no idea how to do this until introduced to the video editing software Camtasia.[1] Camtasia is a screen recorder and video editor software that will allow you to do all the aforementioned four steps.

Figure 10.1   Blended learning. (From Shutterstock.)

It takes some training to learn how to use it, and I suggest having an instructional designer[2] help you through the learning process.

Figure 10.2 is me recording my first video lecture, my voice, and my PowerPoint slides. The result is a published video lecture that was uploaded into the university's learning management system (LMS)[3] for downloading by my students. My three-credit undergraduate course, Introduction to Criminalistics, ended up having 81 video clips, a majority of them video lectures. Creating these video clips is referred to as chunking. Chunking refers to an approach for breaking up more substantial subject matter into smaller units or chunks. The resulting chunks are shorter in duration, approximately 5 to 15 minutes in length that are easier to understand and remember. For example, a typical 1-hour lecture may end up to be broken up into 4 or 5 separate video lectures or chunks. So my 11 three-hour lecture modules became 81 separate video chunks. It sounds like a lot, but remember, after you have committed them to video, it's basically done except for occasional updating of material.

Many faculty members still believe there are negative issues associated with video lectures. For example, they think it is a passive learning

Figure 10.2 Author in his home office studio recording a video lecture.

experience and the video lectures are too long (if you chunk them, that is not a problem), and that there is no engagement between content and the students (in a blended course, you meet with the students in the lab or classroom on a scheduled time frame). Some are concerned that students may not be watching the videos. (My response is to include quizzes after every video lecture.) And finally, they don't know how well the student understands the video lectures. (Practical exercises in the lab or classroom allow students to demonstrate their grasp of the content.)

The positive advantages to video lectures are scheduled video lectures are not hampered by inclement weather, outside commitments, holidays, or even a virus pandemic that shuts down the brick and mortor classroom buildings. The video lectures are viewed on demand by the students 24/7. It forces the student to keep up with the material each week, by only making the content available online during the time period it is assigned. The quality of video content is better and consistent. Video lectures can be viewed multiple times by the student for clarity and accuracy of information.

THE FLIPPED CLASSROOM FORMAT

The *flipped classroom format* is a form of blended learning that flips the traditional relationship between in-class lectures and homework assignments. The students learn new content online by watching video lectures and reading textbook material, usually at home, and what used to be homework is now done in class with teachers offering more personalized guidance and interaction with students instead of lecturing. So students access the course content anytime at home; they can stop, pause, and play the video lectures at their leisure; students can write down questions about the content at home and are already prepared to ask those questions to their teacher. Homework activities are usually exercises that allow the student to demonstrate their grasp of the content they learned in a lecture and textbook readings (Figure 10.3).

It has been my experience after many years of assigning traditional homework assignments that if the student did not understand the content, then they didn't turn in the homework assignment, or it was turned in completely wrong. The result was a low-graded homework assignment that effected their overall grade and a lack of understanding for that particular content. That would be the end of it, and the teacher and student would move on to the next module of learning. With the flipped classroom model, the student receives the content at home, writes down their questions or information they didn't understand, comes into the classroom, and gets the answers to their questions from the teacher. When the students are

Figure 10.3 Teacher in a flipper classroom model assisting a student with a homework assignment in the classroom. (From Shutterstock.)

in the classroom, they commence working on those homework exercises associated with the content they just learned. While the students are working on the homework assignments in class, the teacher is walking around the classroom providing immediate individual attention for the students.

10 Pros and Cons of a Flipped Classroom[4]

Pros	Cons
• Students have more control. • It promotes student-centered learning and collaboration. • Lessons and • content are more accessible (provided there is tech access). • 24/7 access to content. • It can be more efficient with more academic practice.	• It can create or exacerbate a digital divide. • It relies on preparation and trust that the students are watching the videos at home. • There is significant work on the front-end for the teacher. • Not naturally a test-prep form of learning, meaning no teaching to the test. • Time in front of the screens, instead of people and places, is increased.

ASYNCHRONOUS AND SYNCHRONOUS PRESENTATION DELIVERIES

These are two terms that you will become familiar with when considering online education and training programs. You need to be able to distinguish them from each other when asked to present a course. The first is *asynchronous* learning or delivery, which is when all your content is prerecorded, allowing the students to complete their work on their own time. There is no scheduled time for them to be online to meet with the instructor or other students in the class. The aforementioned blended learning formats are examples of asynchronous learning. The student communicates with the instructor electronically.

The second term is *synchronous* learning or delivery. The best way to describe this method is that this delivery is in real time in which a group of students is engaged in learning at the same time, usually with an instructor presenting live online lectures. The instructor may or may not be able to see the students on the screen. At the very minimum the instructor views a list of the student's names in a drop-down screen window and when a student wants to ask a question or make a comment, the student clicks on an icon representing a raised hand and the instructor recognizes the student and responds to their question or comment. The instructor can control what the students see and hears, and all can see and hear each other if the instructor so desires.

Any of the aforementioned methods for delivering content can use a combination of both asynchronous and synchronous presentation delivery methods. I will tell you it has been my experience that any requirement for students to be at a particular location (like a classroom) or a computer (or any mobile device) at a predetermined time is not what today's learners prefer.

During the conavirus pendemic that occurred in the middle of the spring 2020 semseter, I used a combination of asynchronous and synchronous delivery. I already had my asynchronous lectures and etextbook content online with quizzes attached to each module. Once a week, on the day the students were required to take their quiz, I conducted a synchronous live class session where any of the students who wanted to ask me questions, could do so at that time. For the students who could not make that time of the day, the event was recorded and students could view the session at their leisure. Each recorded session was sitting on the course website homepage. Unfortunately, I had to eliminate the in lab class practical exercises.

PRESENTING TO THE CAMERA

I mentioned earlier that what I loved about teaching and public speaking, in general, was speaking before a live audience or lecture hall full of students. Smiling faces looking up at you on the podium give you a high that motivates you to perform at your best. So how did I deal with presenting to the camera instead? It wasn't easy at first, but I knew I had to show the same nonverbals that I did when in the lecture hall. Many of my colleagues who are using some form of blended learning are not using their camera to allow students to view them on the screen while lecturing. So what do those students see? A still of some PowerPoint slide. I am in total disagreement with that decision. I refer you back to Chapter 7, which discussed the use of nonverbal communications and all the reasons why facial expressions, eye contact, gestures, and the tone of your voice play a vital role in the communication process. My students have told me that having my video lectures online is like having their very own personal instructor at home with them.

When lecturing to the camera, you must visualize in the present all those hundreds and possibly thousands of students who will be viewing you in the future. In Figure 10.2, I am doing that, recording 1 of the 81 video chunks for my Introduction to Criminalistics course, today; a blended learning–flipped classroom delivered course. By the way, for every video chuck recorded, I redid it several times over until it was as perfect as I could get it.[5] I forgot that I was alone in my home office studio and imagined that as I looked at the computer monitor with one of my PowerPoint slides on it and the video camera positioned just above, I could visualize those students. It didn't take long for me to comfortably sit there in my studio and talk, minus the physical movement around the room that I was used to doing in the lecture hall. By the way, looking straight ahead at the monitor with the video camera above, as shown in Figure 10.2, projects an image at the receiving end that you are looking right at the student. It gives a personal touch that can never be duplicated in a classroom or a large lecture hall.

For those of you are still not convinced, you may be close enough to retirement not to be forced to change. But for those readers who are sitting on the generation line, be prepared to hear "Lights! Camera! Action!"

CHAPTER REVIEW REFLECTION TOOLS

1. Blended (hybrid) learning is a formal education program in which a student learns at least in part through online delivery of content and instruction with some element of student control over time, place, and pace.

2. The flipped classroom format is a form of blended learning that flips the traditional relationship between class time and homework.
3. Asynchronous delivery, which is when all your content is prerecorded, allows students to complete their work on their own time.
4. Synchronous delivery is done live when a group of students is engaged in learning at the same time, usually with an instructor presenting live online lectures.
5. Presenting to the camera when recording lectures, you must visualize in the present all those hundreds and possibly thousands of students who will be viewing you in the future.
6. Creating short video clips is referred to as chunking. Chunking refers to an approach for breaking up more substantial subject matter into smaller units or chunks.

NOTES

1. TechSmith® Camtasia is one of many video editing software products that can satisfy this requirement. Camtasia is the only one the author has experience with and has used to date.
2. An instructional designer is an education professional whose job is to assist educators in redesigning courses, developing entire courses or curriculums, and creating training materials, such as teaching manuals and student guides. They are also proficient in transforming live lectures into video clips and, if necessary, teaching instructors to do this for themselves.
3. A learning management system (LMS) is a software application or web-based technology used to plan, implement, and assess a specific learning process. It provides an instructor with a way to create and deliver content, monitor student participation, and assess student performance. It is like a website for a course. Examples of LMSs are Blackboard®, Instructure's Canvas, eFRont, and Absorb.
4. TeachThought Staff, "10 Pros and Cons of a Flipped Classroom," January 28, 2019, www.teachthought.com/learning/10-pros-cons-flipped-classroom/.
5. It should be mentioned that unlike live lectures where you say it once, and the listener either gets it right or not, when your lectures are recorded, your students have the opportunity to replay your lecture as many times as they want. You, the instructor can never say I didn't say that because they have you on tape. So you better have it right, because your students will call you on it every time.

Part III

Evaluating and Fine-Tuning Your Performance

Chapters in Part III include the use and evaluation of speaker performance feedback surveys; dealing with the fear of public speaking (glossophobia); using the information in this book to improve speaking skills that eliminate stage fright; and how to practice, seek further formal training, and consider joining Toastmasters International, a nonprofit educational organization that teaches public speaking and leadership skills through a worldwide network of clubs and educational programs.

11

Evaluating Your Presentation Performance

INTRODUCTION

Chapter 11 focuses on the speaker's performance and how best to evaluate their performance. It has been my experience that the only person who really cares about the speaker's performance and development is the speaker. Although there are many speaker evaluation systems out there used by academic and training organizations, few read them and act on them. Therefore, this chapter provides methods for the speaker to seek both positive and negative feedback for the opportunity to learn from the feedback and develop into an accomplished speaker. The reader is reminded of the quote by Dale Carnegie, in the "Preface" of this book: "Great public speakers are not born; they are trained." Therefore, performance feedback surveys are vital to the future success of a well-trained developing speaker (Figure 11.1).

No one likes to be told that they are not liked by someone for who they are or what they did. We live in a society where we generally tell people how great they are or what a great job they did even if that is not the case. Whether it is accurate or not doesn't matter, because nobody wants to hurt anybody's feelings. We want to build their self-confidence and have them feel good about themselves. In so many ways, that is a positive gesture and can result in a positive outcome. But does it help a person's self-development? We tend to reward *participation* in the same manner

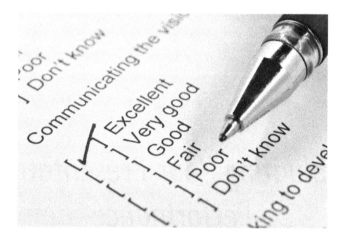

Figure 11.1 Check off performance survey. (From Shutterstock.)

as we reward *performance*. Some schools have stopped *grading* academic work and now list the task as *completed*. Many times, the students don't know if their work was correct or not. In the professional adult world, we are constantly judged and graded. This is how we attain employment, promotions, bonuses, certifications, academic degrees, and demonstrate proficiency in our chosen field of expertise.

So let's discuss how to do this in our public speaking careers, because if you haven't recognized it yet, public speaking is a career field. "A career is often composed of the jobs held, titles earned and work accomplished over a long period of time, rather than just referring to one position."[1] That is why public speaking skills should be developed in the same way as you have done with your chosen career. You didn't wake up one morning and find that you were in expert in your field. You worked at it. You trained and practiced it, made mistakes, adjusted your performance because of those mistakes, and eventually become an expert. This is what you need to do with your public speaking capabilities. Allow yourself to be evaluated so you can identify your mistakes, to learn from them and grow into your true potential as a speaker. You have to be strong and know that everyone is not going to be kind in their evaluation of you. You may even find that some things that people didn't like about you are the very things others liked. Don't forget the 20/60/20 rule discussed in Chapter 3. No matter how good your presentation is, 20% of your audience will not like you, 60% could go either way, and 20% will love you.

A SELF-EVALUATION OF YOUR PRESENTATION SKILLS

It is helpful to self-evaluate your existing skills to be a more effective speaker. Review the following steps to speech development and determine to what extent you are following these steps:

1. I establish basic objectives before planning my presentation.
2. I determine the needs and expectations of my audience.
3. I always develop a strong introduction to grab my audience at the beginning of my presentation.
4. My conclusion summarizes both the introduction and body of my presentation.
5. My visuals augment my spoken word and are not used to replace what I am saying.
6. I ensure that the audience understands the benefits of the information presented clearly and compellingly.
7. I communicate ideas in a motivating, inspiring, and enthusiastic manner.
8. I visit the room where I am speaking ahead of time to ensure the seating, lighting, and audio/visual equipment are in order.
9. I use breaks effectively to allow the audience to refocus.
10. I read, pay attention, and adjust as needed to audience performance evaluation feedback.

Although there is so much more to public speaking addressed throughout this book, these 10 steps are the necessary foundational activities to becoming an excellent speaker. Now let's discuss audience evaluations. It has been my experience that the completion of participant evaluations is done more as a matter of protocol than a tool to evaluate the success of a presentation or to provide feedback to the presenter. Over the years that I have been speaking professionally, if I don't specifically ask to review the evaluation forms completed by my audiences, I would never see them.

HOW TO CREATE AN EVALUATION FORM

The evaluation form is titled in several different ways. It may be referred to as a "Participant Feedback Summary," "Speaker's Evaluation," "Event Evaluation," "Guest Speaker Evaluation Form," or "Program Evaluation." The form should evaluate four aspects of the presentation: the *organization*, its *value* to the audience, the *speaker*, and the *facility* where it was presented. The internet is full of sample templates of these forms to assist

Figure 11.2 An evaluation form. (From Shutterstock.)

you in creating your own (Figure 11.2). The following are questions that represent the four areas to be evaluated that will give the reviewer a clear sense of the success or failure of a presentation or program. As a speaker, it is also essential for you to know how you will be evaluated:

1. Organization
   - Were the objectives of the speech discussed?
   - Were the objectives achieved?
   - Did the presentation cover the topics you expected it to include?
   - Was the subject matter presented adequately?
   - Was the presentation well planned and organized?
2. Value
   - How valuable were the ideas and concepts to you?
   - Would you recommend this presentation to others?
   - Was the presentation appropriately targeted to the particular audience?
   - What topic(s) would you like to add or delete in a future presentation in this subject?
   - How would you improve this presentation or event?
   - What one idea can you best use from the presentation?

3. Speaker
  - Overall rating (quantitative response).
  - Expressed ideas clearly (quantitative response).
  - Enthusiasm for subject (quantitative response).
  - Knowledge of subject (quantitative response).
  - Presentation well organized (quantitative response).
  - How effective was the speaker's presentation of the material?
  - How effective was the use of handouts?
  - How effective was the use of visuals?
  - What was the speaker's major strength?
  - What was the speaker's major weakness?
  - Would you like to hear this speaker again?
4. Facility (all quantitative responses)
  - Event location.
  - Were the chairs comfortable?
  - Was the furniture arranged appropriately for the event?
  - Was the lighting OK?
  - Were you able to view the screen clearly?
  - Were they any distractions in the room?
  - Were you able to hear the speaker clearly?
  - Did the audio/visual equipment work as expected?

*Additional comments – Indicate any other comments that may help the speaker improve the presentation.

HOW TO BENEFIT FROM EVALUATION SURVEY DATA

If you want to benefit from the required data in an evaluation survey, you need to allow the audience to fill out the survey form during your time, not theirs. Don't wait for your time to be up and their time to leave to expect the audience to stay any longer. Most will not. Also, sending the form electronically to audience participants after the presentation is a mistake. You want their immediate feedback while your presentation is fresh in their minds. You must convince the audience that the survey is important to you and the organization hosting the event. Whether the survey responses are good, bad, or indifferent, they will benefit the future presentations and ensure their participation in future presentations you give will be that much better. If you are within your time frame, and you are asking the audience to now fill out the forms before the presentation is concluded, they will naturally do it.

So what do you do with the information? Review the positive as well as negative comments. It is important to know what the audience liked about your presentation. It may have been your style, presentation, your content, or organization. Whatever it was, you probably want to keep it into your repertoire of speaking skills. Study the feedback to see what you did well, what you could have done differently, and what ideas you have developed from the experience for future events. For example, did your accent get in the way of a respondent's understanding of what you were saying? When I first moved away from my home state of Massachusetts, my Boston accent was a distraction for many in my audience. Most would say they liked hearing the Boston accent and would chat with their neighbors in the audience about how I said certain words. Those participants entertained by my accent were being distracted from what I was saying and didn't even notice. Others provided feedback to me that it was a slight problem. After living away from the Boston area for the past 46-plus years, this problem has significantly lessened but has not been eliminated.

I have received evaluation feedback about my loud voice; that it is too loud and again distracting to them. Just remember the 20/60/20 rule. No matter how good you are as a speaker, 20% will not like you, 60% don't care either way, and 20% will like you no matter what you do or say. The 20% who don't like you may feel that for reasons that have nothing to do with your speaking skills, so don't concern yourself with them. Learn and grow with the constructive feedback that has been shared and it will make a positive difference for you.

CHAPTER REVIEW REFLECTION TOOLS

1. The only person who cares about the speaker's performance and development is the speaker.
2. If you want to benefit from the required data in an evaluation survey, you need to allow the audience enough time to fill out the survey form during your time, not theirs.
3. Remember, 20% of your audience won't like you.
4. Remember, 20% of your audience will always like you.

NOTE

1. Business Dictionary, "Career," www.businessdictionary.com/definition/career.html.

12

Presentation Problems and Solutions

INTRODUCTION

Chapter 12 deals with two issues that are prevalent when performing a speech to a live audience. The first is the most difficult one to overcome and that is the fear of public speaking or more commonly called stage fright. The technical term is *glossophobia*. This chapter provides suggestions on how to overcome this sometimes-debilitating phobia by reviewing the content in the previous chapters in this book. The second issue is the recognition that your presentations may be boring and may have received negative feedback from participant evaluations or directly from past taskers. This chapter discusses the characteristic features of the worst and most ineffective presentations and addresses the 10 most common presentation mistakes that can be improved upon to make a positive difference. The 10 areas for improvement are lack of preparation, poor use of visuals, inappropriate humor, inappropriate dress, not knowing the audience, malfunctioning equipment, starting or ending a presentation late, using a monotone voice, too much material in too short a time, and not clarifying the topic.

FEAR OF PUBLIC SPEAKING

Glossophobia, or fear of public speaking, also referred to as stage fright, is a common form of anxiety. It can range from slight nervousness to paralyzing fear and panic when placed in the position to speak in public in any forum. The fear of public speaking is the number one phobia in America. Jerry Seinfeld, renown American comedian, mentions this issue in one of his standup shows when he said, "I saw a thing, actually a study that said speaking in front of a crowd is considered the number one fear of the average person. I found that amazing. Number two was death. Death is number two? This means, to the average person, if you have to be at a funeral, you would rather be in the casket than doing the eulogy."[1] In Rebecca Lake's article "Fear of Public Speaking Statistics and How to Overcome Glossophobia,"[2] she found that it is estimated that as much as 75% of the population struggles with a fear of public speaking to some degree; women more than men are likely to be fearful, and there is a slight racial divide with 43% of whites admitting to being jittery about public speaking versus 34% of nonwhites. What this means and what we can do about it is the focus of this section (Figure 12.1).

If we believe that 75% of the population has some degree of fear when speaking in public, then that in itself should make you feel a little better. It is OK. It is not unusual for you to feel that way.

Many famous people have suffered from glossophobia, including actors, politicians and even presidents. Some notable examples are Renée Zellweger, Nicole Kidman, Abraham Lincoln, Gandhi, Sigmund Freud and Thomas Jefferson. At some point, they all mention actually going out of their way to avoid speaking in public. One extreme case was Gandhi. According to an article in The Atlantic, Gandhi was due to be speaking in a court and only managed to say the first sentence of his speech before

Figure 12.1 Glossophobia. (From Shutterstock.)

he dried up and an assistant stepped in and finished the speech for him. They have all had to devise strategies for overcoming this fear.[3]

Why? Why does this feeling of anxiety and fear allow us to be apprehensive about our ability to be successful? No matter how knowledgeable you are about a topic, that does not naturally give you the skills to publicly speak on the topic. Some can easily discuss a topic with one other person in the room. You add one more person to the group, and everything changes. For these people, it goes from a discussion to a public discourse. It is hard for me to understand this because it has never happened to me, but I do know how real it is for some. I have coached many of my staff members and others who were willing to call in sick, change jobs, or quit a leadership position before speaking publicly about a subject they knew but were not willing to go that extra step. Whatever the cause of this stage fright, be assured that it is not an emotional weakness or personality flaw. It is as common as a cold and as real as a morning hangover. Understand that good speakers are not born, they are made; so let's discuss how to reduce the fear and for many of you eliminate it forever.

A little apprehension is reasonable to experience when preparing to speak in public. It keeps you sharp and focused. You don't want to be too self-confident, so you don't prepare adequately. For example, experiencing butterflies in your stomach is not a bad thing, as long as you keep them flying together in some formation. (See Figures 12.2 to 12.4.)

I have an excellent way to help yourself regain confidence when you are speaking and not sure if your audience is happy with you. In every audience, there is always at least one person that when you make eye contact with them, they immediately smile at you and begin nodding their head up and down in positive recognition. They are saying to you in a nonverbal manner, "Yes! I agree with you!" "Yes! You are right!" "I like you!" "You are good!" I guarantee you that their smiling face and positive gesturing will help you immensely. Seek those people out. They are your friends. There is usually more than one of them, so look around. They are there. I promise you.

The Three Rules for Conquering the Fear

- Have a plan.
- Know your subject, and if you don't know your subject have a plan.
- Rehearse.

Figure 12.2   Fear: Butterflies flying in different directions. (From Shutterstock.)

Figure 12.3   An example of positive development. (From Shutterstock.)

Figure 12.4 Confidence: Butterflies flying in the same direction. (From Shutterstock.)

Having a plan is one of the most important things you can do to conquer your fear of public speaking. It has been my experience that a significant reason for nervousness among new speakers, especially if they don't know how to start the process is that they haven't received any training, and their management doesn't offer any guidance.[4] The idea that the speaker knows the subject is enough for some to believe that is all they need. They have no idea on how to approach the preparation and delivery of a speech, so the fear of the unknown overshadows all the rest of the process. Part I of this book eliminates those concerns.

Knowing your subject is obviously essential, but don't forget Aristotle's notion, "It is not enough to know what to say; one must know how to say it." Sometimes you need to rely on technique rather than subject knowledge. Of course, you should know your subject, and Roger E. Axtell, author of the book *Do's and Taboos of Public Speaking*, makes that point stating, "Know *when* to speak but also *when not* to speak. Speak *only* when you know the subject. *Decline* to speak if you are unsure about or unprepared for the topic."[5] I don't argue that Axtell's suggestion is valid and makes sense, but tell that to your boss when they direct you to give a briefing on a subject you are not comfortable with or say that to your high school principal when they tell you to transform your biology course into a forensic science course and you have no background or experience in the forensic sciences. What do you do then?

STORYTELLING

On December 24, 1997, in my home state of Massachusetts, my 12-year-old nephew, Brian, my sister's son, was accidentally shot by his friend who was showing off his mother's handgun. Brian's friend thought that he had removed all the rounds from the revolver, but one remained stuck in the cylinder. He pulled the trigger three times to hear the click, click, click, but on the third click the gun fired and struck Brian. He passed away hours later in a local hospital on Christmas Eve night. It was a devastating time for our family.

The night before the funeral, while at the funeral home during the "viewing," my sister asked me if I would deliver the eulogy at the church the following morning. Although I had delivered eulogies for both my grandparents, this was not the same. I, of course, told my sister that I would do the tribute, but I had no idea how to start.

My public speaking books, slides, and notes were all at home in Maryland. This was a time before the internet was there to help. I walked around in the funeral home, trying to figure out how to prepare to give a speech without any preparation or real knowledge about who Brian was as a person that I would be eulogizing the following day. Living in Maryland, I only saw Brian for short periods during the holidays. But all of a sudden I remembered something … something that I had been teaching in my public speaking workshop for years. It was the image of one of my 35mm slides that ended up my savior. (See Figure P1.1, A communication model.) I had this slide etched in my brain from presenting the workshop so many times in the past.

I started with the tasker, my sister, and asked her what she wanted those who would be attending the funeral to hear about Brian. Although Brian was the subject of the eulogy, the family and friends he left behind were my audience. They were the ones I needed to satisfy. So by talking to his mom and dad, siblings, grandparents, extended family and friends, the introduction, body, and summary of my speech was completed. I also used text from sympathy cards sent to my sister and notes left behind by Brian's friends that provided insight into a young man who was loved by those he touched. These two sources of information proved to be valuable when searching for the right words to share with those who attended the funeral.

This one slide is an example of how one piece of information made a difference to having a plan. The anxiety I was experiencing at the beginning subsided, except for the sorrow and grief we all would be feeling for a long time afterward.

Another example for when you are forced to speak on a subject you are not entirely knowledgeable about is to invite "subject matter experts" familiar with your topic to attend your presentation. Introduce them to your audience and tell them that you have them there because you want to ensure the audience is receiving the most accurate information possible. Don't tell them it's because you haven't got a clue about what you are talking about. And of course, don't apologize for not having a clue; they don't want to hear excuses. They want to hear factual information, and it doesn't matter to them who gives it to them.

Rehearse is a much gentler word than the word practice. Both words mean the same, but rehearsing reminds us of the entertaining profession, and a presentation is always successful when it is perceived as entertainment. So rehearse your speech until you have it right. Have what, right? Your timing for one. Making sure you have enough content to fill the time you have allotted to you and then review the content of your presentation together with your slides to ensure that you have the appropriate number of slides necessary to augment what you will be saying. Also, rehearse your transitions from one topic to the next.

The logistics for a presentation can be the cause of more anxiety then the presentation itself. Is the room conducive to how you want to present your material? That includes the tables, chairs, lighting, and positioning of the projection screen. Have you checked all the equipment in the room and made sure that if you are using your personal laptop, that it connects properly with the system installed in the room? I always find time before I am speaking to go to the place where I will be speaking. I set up all my equipment to make sure everything works; run through all my slides, video and audio clips; and check on the microphone to ensure it works and is loud enough to be heard. I move around the room and go to the farthest distance away from the screen to see what my slides look like, if they can be easily read, and if I can hear the audio comfortably.

Although you can rehearse your material at home or in the office, the rehearsal done in the room where you will be speaking will reduce some of that anxiety you might experience otherwise. I believe that much of the anxiety speakers experience comes from thinking about the unknown. Whether you have spoken in the room before or not, acquainting yourself with the room before the audience comes in can reduce a lot of that anxiety. If you are there before your audience, then the audience is coming into your house instead of you entering when the audience is there already, and you are entering their house.

Every speech is a new experience, similar to a new job. When you first begin a new job that requires new knowledge, you are a little apprehensive and nervous until you do it a few times, feel more comfortable with it, and when you have done it enough, it becomes second nature to you. Many speeches are one-time performances, so you don't get the opportunity to experience the learning process in the same way. Therefore, rehearing it before presenting it is what you need to do to get yourself at a level of comfort and confidence. So if you take the time to rehearse, you will be glad you did.

MY PRESENTATION IS BORING

Why, of course, it is. If you think your presentation is boring, and you are bored delivering it, then your presentation is boring. You may even have received some negative feedback in a performance review from a previous delivery of the presentation as further evidence. Simple deductive reasoning my dear Watson, if A = B and B = C, then A = C. But you are halfway there to fixing the problem because you have recognized you have a problem. Good for you. You must have jumped ahead in this book and when this section appeared before your eyes, you thought the answer was here. Well, it is not. Your solution to fix the problem is spread throughout the chapters in Part I, but let's discuss the issue before you go back there (Figure 12.5).

> If you're giving a presentation and you're not interested, how can your audience be interested? You've got to figure out the story of what you've done and tell it in a way that is interesting and enthusiastic. In other words, you really have to show up for your audience. I would say that selling your science is at least half of the work that you do and how successful you will be.
>
> – Jill Bolte Taylor[6]

206

Figure 12.5   Boring your audience. (From Shutterstock.)

Tell stories to make highly scientific and technical points to your audience. It will make your presentation more engaging and memorable and easier to understand. Inject humor whenever it is appropriate to grab your audience's attention and keep them interested in hearing your next point of information. Be careful not to present too much statistical data at once. Spread it out evenly with other information that will be valued by the audience. That is why knowing your audience is so important. How important is it for the audience to have all those boring statics and graphs in your presentation? That information may be relevant to you and your research, but how necessary is it for the audience to view it? Be clear on what your objectives are and what you are trying to achieve.

DOS AND DON'TS

The following dos and don'ts are repeated essential points made throughout the book and are also listed as "Reflection Tools" found at the end of each chapter (Figure 12.6).

During Preparation

DO speak personally with the individual who requested the presentation to determine the objectives.

Figure 12.6 Dos and don'ts. (From Shutterstock.)

DON'T allow a third party to interpret them for you.

DO begin the presentation task by writing down a few short bullets that best describe the objectives. These objectives will be the framework of the entire presentation.

DON'T start collecting data until your objectives are clear in your mind.

DO find out as much about the audience as possible.

DON'T ever give a presentation without knowing your audience ahead of time.

DO write your presentation outline notes first before considering the use of PowerPoint slides and other visual aids.

DON'T create your presentation around your slides. The slides should only augment what you will be saying.

Prior to the Presentation

DO consider the presentation room setup, furniture, audiovisual equipment, and availability.

DON'T go into the room without having prepared it ahead of time.

DO determine who will introduce you and introduce the topic on your presentation.

DON'T begin a presentation without having the audience provided with an introduction to you and your topic.

DO tell your audience how long you will be speaking and when the breaks will come.

DON'T speak for more than 60 to 75 minutes without a break and DON'T go over the time you told them you would finish.

DO consider the use of handouts or other supporting materials.

DON'T pass out material unless it has a purpose and further clarifies your presentation.

Delivery Techniques

DO move around at the podium to allow your audience to move their heads a little.

DON'T stay still behind the lectern. It bores your audience and tends to put them to sleep.

DO use hand gestures and voice variations as methods to emphasize a point and keep your audience awake.

DON'T put your hands in your pocket, or hold on to the lectern, and DON'T use a monotone voice. It is a hypnotic and unemotional tone that will also put your audience asleep.

DO ask thought-provoking questions of your audience. It gets them involved and thinking.

DON'T point at anyone to answer the question; let them volunteer. DON'T answer the question for them without waiting for at least 10 seconds. This will give them enough time to formulate a response. You see, they have to hear you ask the question, think about an answer, decide if they want to respond, and then raise their hand. That requires at least 10 seconds, which feels like a lifetime for you, the speaker.

Visual Aids

DO use visuals to augment what you are communicating.

DON'T use word slides that either state verbatim what you are already saying orally, or DON'T add clarity to what you are already saying.

DO make sure that the slides are simple and can be seen and read by the audience in the back row.

DON'T use slides that are dark, busy, or contain confusing diagram visuals.

DO use the 6/30 formula when deciding the number of slides for your presentation. (Six slides per 30 minutes of presentation time.)

DON'T feel a need to have a slide for every point being made.

DO consider using a video clip with your presentation to widen the sphere of view.

DON'T use a video that is any more than 5 to 10 minutes in length.

CHAPTER REVIEW REFLECTION TOOLS

1. Glossophobia, or fear of public speaking, also referred to as stage fright, is a common form of anxiety.
2. A little apprehension is reasonable to experience when preparing to speak in public. It keeps you sharp and focused.
3. The three rules for conquering the fear: have a plan, know your subject, and rehearse.
4. If you think your presentation is boring, and you are bored delivering it, then your presentation is boring.
5. Tell stories to make highly scientific and technical points to your audience. It will make your presentation more engaging and memorable and easier to understand.

NOTES

1. Jerry Seinfeld, excerpt from "I'm Telling You For The Last Time" performance, January 26, 2014.
2. Rebecca Lake, "Fear of Public Speaking Statistics and How to Overcome Glossophobia," CreditDonkey, April 28, 2015, www.creditdonkey.com/fear-of-public-speaking-statistics.html.
3. Ros and Neil Johnson, "How to Overcome Your Fear of Public Speaking," British Council Worldwide+, October 10, 2016, www.britishcouncil.org/voices-magazine/how-overcome-fear-public-speaking.
4. On April 8, 2010, the University of Maryland approved five goals set forth in the "Transforming General Education – A Strategic Plan for a New Vision." The first goal was "students will develop the skills necessary to succeed in academic careers and in professional lives by establishing habits and

understanding of clear writing, effective speaking and presentation, and critical and analytic reasoning." This has made a positive difference for our graduates who now graduate with communication skills they never had before.

5. Roger E. Axtell, *Do's and Taboos of Public Speaking: How to Get Those Butterflies Flying in Formation*, John Wiley & Sons, 1992, p. 11.
6. As quoted in Michael Alley, *The Craft of Scientific Presentation: Critical Steps to Succeed and Critical Errors to Avoid*, 2nd ed., Springer, 2013, p. 35.

13

Developing Your Public Speaking Skills

INTRODUCTION

Chapter 13 provides direction for the reader on how to develop their skills in the area of public speaking. The author discusses the importance of practice, rehearsal, and reviewing the basic principles presented in this book; and suggests attending public speaking workshops and academic courses, and online programs. The author's most significant suggestion is to become a member and participate in Toastmasters International, a nonprofit educational organization that teaches public speaking through a worldwide network of local clubs.

The "Preface" of this book clearly states that great speakers are not born; they are made. Therefore, like any other skill we perfect during our lives, public speaking skills have to be learned. Do some great speakers have innate qualities that make it easier for them to achieve success? Qualities include being uninhibited, outgoing, enjoying being the center of attention, comfortable in groups, and confident in their profession. Yes, of course, but that doesn't eliminate the need for them to learn and practice the skills outlined in this book. You have to recognize that public speaking like any other professional skill needs training, experience, practice, adjustment, more training, more experience, more practice, a willingness to make mistakes and learn from those mistakes, and then fine-tuning the knowledge, skills. and abilities you obtain that makes you all that you can be as a public speaker.

Figure 13.1 Speaker at lectern. (From Shutterstock.)

Whether you are speaking to one or one thousand people, have never spoken in public before, or have been speaking in public for years and think you are good at it; however you fit in any of these scenarios, developing your public speaking skills should be a work in progress. Some things will stay the same, such as the physical ability of your audience to see messages with their eyes, hear with their ears, and understand and remember with their brains. But how you transmit those messages, and how they receive and retain those messages are always changing and being redeveloped. PowerPoint alone has had a far-reaching effect on speech delivery. Computers, audiovisual hardware and software, social media, the internet, and YouTube have all revolutionized how we get information across to our audiences and is always changing.

The ability to speak in public is a tool used by a criminal justice professional far more than their weapon or wit. More disturbance calls have been resolved with the power of what comes out of the officer's mouth rather than what is encountered with their fist. Attorneys have won more cases with their ability to persuade juries with their words rather than any physical evidence introduced.

There are so many ways for you to develop your skills, so I am listing them here, so there are no excuses for not knowing what you can do next.

READ THIS BOOK

You acquired this book, and that was a great beginning. I highly suggest you read it cover to cover. Then as you get public speaking opportunities, read it cover to cover again. Pay particular attention to the "Reflection Tools" at the end of each chapter. They review the critical learning skills for each chapter. You will notice that many of these skills and tools are repeated over and over again throughout the book. That is because repetition is key to help you remember.

WORKSHOPS

Professional conferences usually have a series of workshops at the beginning of the week of a conference event. Public speaking workshops are generally three to four hours in duration, and provide an opportunity to improve your presentation skills through strategic planning, preparation, and performance. I have been teaching such a workshop titled "Motivation through Communications – A Briefing Skills Presentation," since I first created it in the early 1980s. The workshop presents techniques for speaking in all settings with confidence, choosing the right audiovisual technologies, and dealing with questions from an audience. Fifty-five proven effective presentation tools are presented, demonstrated, and provided to each participant who attends this workshop.

FREE ONLINE MATERIAL

Today's generations do not recognize how fortunate they are to have all the free content available to them on any subject they want at their fingertips. While writing this book, I was amazed at how much content there was on public speaking out there on the information highway. There are articles, PowerPoint slides shows, video clips, written speeches, blogs, and free short training sessions (Figure 13.2).

ONLINE TRAINING

The following are just a few online training programs that are available to know what is out there:

- eCornell, "STAND APART – Executive Presence Certificate from Cornell University"[1]

Figure 13.2 Search online public speaking training and content. (From Shutterstock.)

- By sharing videos of yourself presenting and receiving constructive feedback from fellow students and experts, you'll practice analyzing your performance, repeating and refining your work in exercises and acting techniques specially designed by Cornell theatre professor David Feldshuh.
- Analyze and understand your strengths and weaknesses as a presenter.
- Connect and affect listeners when you transfer information, share emotion, or persuade for change.
- Observe and appreciate the performance aspects in others and learn how these insights can contribute to your presence.
- Deal with performance anxiety, mannerisms, and other distractions that limit your effectiveness in presentation.
- Create a self-training process using self-video, self-analysis, focused exercises, and rubric assessment to continue improvement after the course is completed.
- Udemy, "Presentation Skills Courses."[2] Courses include:
  - The Complete Presentation and Public Speaking/Speech Course
  - Confidence On Camera: Make Amazing Videos, Easily.
  - Public Speaking and Presentations Pro: No Beginners Allowed!

- Complete Presentation Skills Masterclass for Every Occasion
- Presenting with Confidence: Prepare, Practice, and Perform!
- Class Central, University of Washington via Coursera, "Introduction to Public Speaking"[3]
  - Syllabus
    - Week 1: Understanding speech
    - Week 2: Making ideas compelling and memorable
    - Week 3: Illustrating and delivering your ideas
    - Week 4: Overcoming your fear of public speaking and developing great delivery
    - Week 5: Course conclusion and your final speech

ACADEMIC COLLEGE COURSES

Just about all community colleges and universities offer academic credit courses on public speaking. Some major courses of study require it, but too many of them do not. I am happy to say that the University of Maryland, where I have been teaching since 1977, has an oral communications course requirement for all undergraduate students. My recommendation to any college students reading this book is not to let this opportunity pass you by; take public speaking as an elective, rather than bowling or basket weaving.

JOIN A PUBLIC SPEAKERS CLUB

If you are serious about developing your speaking skills and want to be considered a professional speaker, in the same fashion as you believe yourself a criminal justice professional or any other professional, this is how you can do it in an environment that offers you training, practice, evaluation, fellowship, competition, and fun. Join the only public speakers club I am aware of, join *Toastmasters International*.

Join Your Local Toastmasters International Club

Toastmasters International is a nonprofit educational organization that teaches public speaking and leadership skills through a worldwide network of clubs. Headquartered in Englewood, Colo., the organization's membership exceeds 358,000 in more than 16,800 clubs in 143 countries. Since 1924, Toastmasters International has helped people from diverse backgrounds become more confident speakers, communicators, and leaders.[4]

Go online to find the closest club in your area. It could be a local community club or a club located right in your own employer's facility. Most federal government agencies have approved Toastmasters clubs to be recognized in their facilities and have allowed paid time off to attend a one-hour meeting session per week. I know; I was a member of my agency's local club for over five years. I not only attended meetings, but I also gave some of my staff opportunities to attend to help them develop their speaking skills. For one of my staff members, I included a requirement in their employee performance plan to attend meetings and required them to complete a certain number of speeches. It was a win-win for the staff member who knew they needed the training, wanted to receive it, and was now able to do so on company time as part of their employee improvement plan.

How does it work?

- Find a club and walk in. Tell the greeter that you a first-time attendee and would like to sit in and see what it is all about. You will be welcomed and introduced to all the members.
- Meetings usually have an average of 5 to 25 members attending at any given time.
- Fill out the membership application and pay the annual dues and new member fees.

What happens at the meetings?

- You receive your first manual that contains 10 speech projects to help you gain the basic skills needed to present an effective speech. Each speech that you give in front of your club members will be from 5 to 7 minutes in length, with specific objectives you are to attain listed in the manual.
- You will give a speech when you believe you are ready, and when that time comes, you will notify the club's Educational Vice President to place you on the meeting schedule in the next available slot.
- At the same time that you are scheduled, another member will be scheduled as your evaluator. Your evaluator will be prepared to give a short speech on how well you did. The evaluator's feedback will always be positive, sharing with you what you did well and what areas you need to work on for improvement.
- There will be several other members presenting a speech at the meeting and having them evaluated.

Meeting roles[5]

- Toastmaster – The Toastmaster is a meeting's director and host.
- Grammarian – The Grammarian helps club members improve their grammar and vocabulary.
- Topicsmaster – The Topicsmaster prepares several "Table Topics," which are one- to five-word phrases from some current event. The idea is to have members practice giving impromptu speeches. The Topicsmaster will select members at random to respond by providing a Table Topics impromptu speech.
- Ah-Counter – The Ah-Counter counts each time any member uses an unnecessary utterance or filler word like "ahs." A report will be given at the end of the meeting on the exact number of utterances made and by whom.
- Timer – The Timer takes on this role to improve time management skills. Each speech is timed using a device with green, yellow, and red lights.
- Speech Evaluator – Speech Evaluators provide verbal and written feedback to meeting speakers.
- General Evaluator – The General Evaluator evaluates how the meeting was conducted using the standards set forth by Toastmasters International.

Look for Opportunities to Speak

Looking for opportunities to speak is the only way to get better. I believe that I have been able to reach a high level of proficiency with public speaking because I do so much of it. I have been able to make every mistake there is to make, learn from it, and then adjust from it. I am always looking for opportunities to speak. I still can't believe that I have been teaching every semester since 1977 and get paid to speak. I get paid while I am learning, you see because I am always learning in this business. I have been fortunate to have been using my skills for criminal justice, forensic sciences, and counterintelligence fields, and so can't you. I believe promotions and special assignments go to those persons whose talents are recognized by senior leadership. There is no better way to be more recognized than to be at the podium, having those assembled pay attention to what you have to say.

My wife and I had the privilege to visit the Ronald Reagan Presidential Library and Museum in Simi Valley, California, in 2017. I was inspired by

Figure 13.3   Reagan Library. (Photo by T.P. Mauriello.)

one of the displays there that was a photograph of President Reagan when he was in college. There was an inscription under his photo that reflected what the young Ronald Reagan experienced when he gave his first speech. The Great Communicator said, "Giving that speech – my first – was as exciting as any I ever gave. For the first time in my life I felt my words reach out and grab an audience, and it was exhilarating." (See Figure 13.3.)

CHAPTER REVIEW REFLECTION TOOLS

1. Developing your public speaking skills should be a work in progress.
2. The ability to speak in public is a tool used by criminal justice professionals far more than their weapon or wit.
3. Join your local Toastmasters International Club.
4. Look for opportunities to speak. That is the only way to get better.

NOTES

1. eCornell, STAND APART – Executive Presence Certificate from Cornell University, is an academic certification program.
2. Udemy, "Presentation Skills Courses," www.udemy.com/topic/presentation-skills/.
3. Class Central, University of Washington via Coursera, Introduction to Public Speaking, www.classcentral.com/course/public-speaking-889.
4. Toastmasters International, "All About Toastmasters," www.toastmasters.org/about/all-about-toastmasters.
5. Toastmasters International, "Club Meeting Roles," www.toastmasters.org/membership/club-meeting-roles.

BIBLIOGRAPHY

*The following are books for further reference and reading suggested by the author:

"The Art of Rhetoric," by Aristotle; translated by H.C. Lawson-Tancred; Penguin Books, 1991.

"Total Recall – How To Maximize Your Memory Power," by Joan Minninger, Ph.D.; MJF Books, 1984.

"Present Yourself!" by Michael J. Gelb; Jalmar Press; 1988.

"The Mind Map Book," by Tony Buzan with Barry Buzan; A Plume Book; 1993.

"Beyond The Podium," by Allison Rossett & Kendra Sheldon; Jossey-Bass/Pfeiffer Books; 2001.

"Scientists Must Speak," by D. Eric Walters and Gale C. Walters, Second Edition; CRC Press, 2011.

"Do's and Taboos of Public Speaking – How to Get Those Buttgerflies Flying in Formation," by Roger E. Axtell; John Wiley & Sons, Inc., 1992.

"Secrets of Successful Speakers – How You Can Motivate, Captivate & Persuade," by Lilly Walters; McGraw-Hill, Inc., 1993.

"The Craft of Scientific Presentations – Critical Steps to Success and Critical Erroes to Avoid," by Michael Alley, Second Edition; Springer, 2013.

"The Basics of Communication – A Relational Perspective," by Steve Duck and David T. McMahan, Second Edition; Sage Publications, Inc., 2012.

"Beyond Bullet Points - Using Microsoft PowerPoint to Create Presentations that Inform, Motivate, and Inspire," by Cliff Atkinson; Microsoft Press, 2005.

"How to Say It Best – Choice Words, Phrases, & Model Speeches for Every Occasion," by Jack Griffin; Prentice Hall, 1994.

INDEX